180
Faith-Building
Prayers

FOR BOYS

180
Faith-Building
Prayers

FOR BOYS

Janice Thompson

BARBOUR BOOKS
An Imprint of Barbour Publishing, Inc.

ISBN 978-1-68322-871-4

Published by Barbour Books, an imprint of Barbour Publishing Inc., 1810 Barbour Drive, Uhrichsville, Ohio 44683, www.barbourbooks.com

Our mission is to inspire the world with the life-changing message of the Bible.

Member of the
Evangelical Christian
Publishers Association

Printed in the United States of America.
06385 0219 SP

INTRODUCTION

God is interested in every single thing you have to say!

In fact, He loves when His kids take the time to talk to Him. You've got a lot on your mind, and His ears are wide open. This devotional prayer book is a great reminder to talk with God about anything and everything. Whether you're happy or sad, up or down, excited or down in the dumps, you'll find prayers in this book that will hit the spot. Each prayer is perfectly paired with a great verse from the Bible—a totally wonderful way for you to begin or end your day.

Quiet time with God is the best! He can't wait to hang out with you. So what's keeping you? Dive on in! Let's start praying.

⊪ BUDDIES ⫽

You've had a lot of friends in your life—some better than others. You know whom you can trust and whom you can't. God wants you to pray for all of your friends, even the ones who bug you. Yep, it's going to be hard, but you can do it!

MY BUDDIES, MY FRIENDS

Jesus, thank You for my friends! The tall ones, short ones, talkative ones, shy ones, goofy ones, quiet ones. . .I love them all, and I'm happy they're in my life. Even on the bad days my buddies know how to make me laugh. When I'm feeling down, they make me forget about my troubles. They tell me jokes, and I can't stop laughing. They act goofy so I won't be upset anymore. Sometimes they just sit and listen when I tell them what I'm going through. I like that best of all. I don't know where I'd be without my friends, Lord. Show me how to be the kind of friend others have been to me so that I can be a shining reflection of You in this world. I want to be the best friend I can be. Amen.

A man of many companions may come to ruin,
but there is a friend who sticks closer than a brother.
PROVERBS 18:24 ESV

DARE TO BE DIFFERENT

I don't know why I work so hard to be like my friends, Lord. You didn't create us to be cookie-cutter creations, after all. (Yum—cookies sound good right now!) What does it really matter if my shoes are a different brand or I wear my hair in a different style? Sometimes it's cooler to stand out in the crowd, to be unique. Give me the courage to be myself. I don't want to be a follower. I want to be a leader, one who dares to be exactly who he's supposed to be. And when others are saying mean or hurtful things to kids around them, I want to act differently. I don't just want to *look* different; I want to *be* different. Help me, I pray. Amen.

Finally, dear brothers and sisters, we urge you in the name of the Lord Jesus to live in a way that pleases God, as we have taught you. You live this way already, and we encourage you to do so even more.

1 THESSALONIANS 4:1 NLT

ACCOUNTABILITY

Sometimes, Lord, I need an accountability partner—someone who holds me responsible, someone who says, "Hey, did you do that thing you said you were gonna do?" I don't always follow through on my own, but with the help of a friend, maybe I'd do a better job. Can You show me which friend would make a good partner? And while we're at it, could You help me be that kind of friend to others? I want to be the sort of person others can turn to when they need a reminder. Most of all, I'm thankful that You hold me accountable, Lord. You're always whispering in my ear, "Hey, remember to clean your room!" or "Don't forget to do your homework." Best accountability partner ever! Amen.

*Brothers, if anyone is caught in any transgression,
you who are spiritual should restore him in a spirit of
gentleness. Keep watch on yourself, lest you too be tempted.
Bear one another's burdens, and so fulfill the law of Christ.*
GALATIANS 6:1–2 ESV

HEALTHY RELATIONSHIPS

Lord, You know I've had a few rocky friendships. There are some boys out there who make things really hard. They tell lies and sometimes do things to hurt me. Some even have a really bad temper. Others pretend to be nice, but they're just faking it. But I'm learning to make good choices, Father! I want to have friends who treat others kindly and who help me grow in my faith. Would You bring new friends like this into my life, Lord? I really need them. Please send me strong guys who will bring out the best in me. I want my relationships to be healthy, Lord, and I want to be the very best friend I can possibly be to others. Amen.

Let your conversation be gracious and attractive so that you will have the right response for everyone.
COLOSSIANS 4:6 NLT

PEER PRESSURE

Dear Lord, I need to talk to You about something. It's something kind of hard. There's stuff going on at school and in my neighborhood. Kids are doing things they shouldn't. And they're trying to talk me into doing the wrong thing too. I don't want to go along with them—I really don't—but sometimes they almost convince me. I know in my heart that it's a bad choice, but I don't want my friends to hate me or kick me out of the group. Today I'm asking You to give me the courage to stand up to them and to be brave. I want to be strong enough to say no to the things that make You sad. What You think about me is so much more important than what my friends think, Father. May I never forget that. Amen.

*Live wisely among those who are not believers,
and make the most of every opportunity.*
COLOSSIANS 4:5 NLT

FRIEND ENVY

I'll admit it, Lord—sometimes I get jealous. In fact, I get so green with envy that I end up angry. Sometimes I'm jealous when my friends hang out with each other but don't include me. Other times I'm jealous because my friend is super-talented, and I don't feel talented at all. I don't like that feeling. Sometimes I wish I had the kind of life that others have. I envy their homes, cars, or vacations. But then You remind me that I'm already blessed. I have all I need and more. There's no point in being jealous of others. I'm grateful for that reminder, Lord, because I don't want to be envious. Help me, please. Amen.

Anger is cruel and fury overwhelming,
but who can stand before jealousy?
PROVERBS 27:4 NIV

THEY'RE PICKING ON ME

It doesn't feel good when people make fun of me, Lord. It hurts my feelings. Sometimes they're joking around. I get that. But that doesn't make it hurt any less. When people say rude things about my hair, my skin, my shoes, my clothes, or the house I live in. . .it really bothers me. When they comment on my grades or my habits, it stings. Help me forgive those people. And may I never be like that! I don't ever want to be the sort of person who makes fun of others or deliberately hurts them. When I see someone struggling to fit in, help me be a friend to the friendless. May everyone know that I care about others. Amen.

*"But I say to you, Love your enemies and
pray for those who persecute you."*
MATTHEW 5:44 ESV

PRAYING FOR YOUR ENEMIES

I don't like having enemies, Lord. In fact, I never thought I would have any. But some of the people I thought I could trust—my friends—have turned out to be enemies. I call them "frenemies," because they still pretend to be my friend some of the time. Today I choose to pray for those who have hurt me. I forgive the ones who've done bad things to me or spoken mean words. Even if we never become true friends, I pray that the bitterness will end. Show us how to treat each other kindly. I know that You prayed for Your enemies, Jesus. If You can do it—especially after how they treated you—then I can too! Amen.

Let love be your guide. Christ loved us and offered his life for us as a sacrifice that pleases God.
EPHESIANS 5:2 CEV

GIRLS WHO ARE FRIENDS

Sometimes girls drive me crazy. They're so. . . different. I don't get them at all. Then, other times, I feel a little jealous. Girls seem to have it easier in many ways. All they have to worry about is goofy stuff like how to wear their hair or how stylish their clothes are. They don't get picked on as much or have to deal with bullies like boys do. At least that's how it seems to me. Some of my friends are really starting to like girls, Lord. They have crushes. I'm glad I don't have to worry about that for a while. I can be friends with a girl, but crushing on her can wait! In the meantime, help me have good relationships with the girls—sisters, cousins, friends, classmates—in my life. Amen.

So God created man in his own image, in the image of God he created him; male and female he created them.
GENESIS 1:27 ESV

BULLIES

They drive me nuts, Lord! Those bullies are a pain. They make life so hard, not just for me, but for my friends and family too. Why do they always act like they're better than others? Why do they push people around? Lord, today I choose to forgive the bullies. I release my resentment of them and trust You to do a work in them. Change them from the inside out. Where there is hatred, teach them to love. Where there is anger, give them peace. In other words, change their hearts, Lord. Show them that they can live good, happy lives without causing pain to others. Thank You in advance. Amen.

*Don't take part in doing those worthless things that
are done in the dark. Instead, show how wrong they are.
It is disgusting even to talk about what is done in the dark.*
EPHESIANS 5:11–12 CEV

⫸ FAMILY ⫷

Parents, siblings, grandparents, aunts, uncles, cousins. . . you're part of a great big family. God didn't place you where you are by accident. Nope! He knew exactly what He was doing! Whether they're goofy, cranky, or wacky, your family members are your people, and they adore you.

THE FAMILY YOU'RE IN

You created families, Lord! What a cool idea! You decided there should be moms, dads, brothers, sisters, cousins, aunts, and uncles. You were especially creative when You thought up grandparents! Sometimes I wonder how I ended up in the family I'm in. I feel different from the others. But You put me here on purpose. I'm surrounded by exactly the right people, even when it doesn't feel like it. Today, please be with people who don't have families— elderly people, orphans, and widows. Show us who we can "adopt" into our family today. Amen.

God sets the lonely in families.
PSALM 68:6 NIV

PARENTS

Lord, I think it's so cool that You decided to place kids in families. If I didn't have a mom or dad, who would have changed my diaper when I was little? Who would have fed me? You gave those jobs to people who love me and want to see me grow up healthy and strong. Have I thanked You lately for my parents? I don't always act like I'm grateful for them, but I am! They do so much for me—they make sure I have a safe place to live, a bed, good food, and clothes to wear. They work hard so that I can have a good life. I'm learning as I watch them. One day I want to be a great parent too. And by the way, thanks for being the very best Dad ever, Lord. Amen!

Children, you belong to the Lord, and you do the right thing when you obey your parents. The first commandment with a promise says, "Obey your father and your mother, and you will have a long and happy life."
EPHESIANS 6:1–3 CEV

GRANDPARENTS

I'm pretty crazy about my grandparents, Lord! It's not just because they sometimes let me get away with things my parents don't. Okay, in all honesty, they do go easier on me! It's mostly because they love hanging out with me. We do such fun things together—play games, go to the park, go out to eat—lots of stuff that makes me happy. Mostly, I love talking to them. Their stories are the best! When they start talking about the things they did when they were kids, I feel like I'm watching a movie. Maybe one day I'll be a grandparent and I'll have cool stories to tell. How awesome would that be? If that happens, I hope I'm as much fun as my grandparents are right now. Thanks for giving them to me, Lord. Amen.

*Grandchildren are the crown of the aged,
and the glory of children is their fathers.*
PROVERBS 17:6 ESV

SIBLINGS

Brothers and sisters can be a real pain. Sometimes they get on my nerves, Lord. Other times they're pretty cool. We play together and get into mischief together, and we're growing up together. I don't know why You chose to place me in the family You did, but it's been pretty exciting. Help me to be the best brother I can be—to my real brothers and sisters and to those who are so close they're almost like family. I want to love others the way You do, Lord. I want to put their needs before my own. This is hard, but I want to give it my best shot. I'll need Your help if I'm going to succeed. May I win the Brother of the Year award! Amen.

Love each other like brothers and sisters. Give each other more honor than you want for yourselves.
ROMANS 12:10 NCV

BLENDED FAMILIES

You sure know how to bring people together, Lord! You can take broken families and mend them. You can bring in new brothers and sisters—halves and steps—and make them all whole. You love when we all live together in peace and harmony. Today I pray for everyone I know in a blended family, with new sisters, brothers, mothers, or fathers. May they all feel a sense of love and belonging. And thank You, Lord, for making us all part of Your family—no matter who we are, where we come from, or what we look like. That makes me happy! Thank You. Amen.

We ought always to give thanks to God for you, brothers, as is right, because your faith is growing abundantly, and the love of every one of you for one another is increasing.
2 THESSALONIANS 1:3 ESV

CHURCH

A good church is like a family, isn't it, Lord? I have brothers and sisters (and tons of parents!) at my church. I'm surrounded on every side. There are people who love me like one of their own, and that feels so good. I love hanging out with the people at church because we can all worship You as one big happy family. And my church is a great community. I feel safe when I'm spending time with people there. Thanks for adding to the family, Lord. Amen.

*And let us consider how to stir up one another to
love and good works, not neglecting to meet together,
as is the habit of some, but encouraging one another,
and all the more as you see the Day drawing near.*
HEBREWS 10:24–25 ESV

DIVORCE

Father, I've seen it so many times: Parents splitting up. Kids getting hurt. Being caught in the middle. It's a terrible thing to have to divide your heart. Today I pray for every friend or loved one who's been through a divorce. For every child who's feeling guilty, who thinks it might be his or her fault, show them it's not. Heal every broken heart. Mend the hurt places. Give peace. Let them know that this isn't the end of a relationship with Mom or Dad, just the beginning of a new and different one. You can mend anything, Lord, even a heart shattered by divorce. Thank You for caring about parents and kids dealing with divorce. Amen.

Two are better than one, because they have a good reward for their toil. For if they fall, one will lift up his fellow. But woe to him who is alone when he falls and has not another to lift him up! Again, if two lie together, they keep warm, but how can one keep warm alone? And though a man might prevail against one who is alone, two will withstand him—a threefold cord is not quickly broken.
ECCLESIASTES 4:9–12 ESV

ONE BIG HAPPY FAMILY

I hear that expression a lot, Lord—"one big happy family." Only, we're not always happy. Seems like someone's always upset or mad. One kid is jealous of the other. Mom's frustrated. Dad's tired from working all day. We have days that totally stink! Then on other days, everything goes right. My brothers and sisters are in a good mood, Mom has a smile on her face, and Dad is happy to have a day off from work. In good times and bad, I know You're there for us, Lord. And in spite of any rough days, we really are one big happy family. . . because we have each other. Thanks for sticking with us, Lord. Amen.

"Your offspring shall be like the dust of the earth, and you shall spread abroad to the west and to the east and to the north and to the south, and in you and your offspring shall all the families of the earth be blessed."
GENESIS 28:14 ESV

DON'T MESS WITH MY FAMILY!

I'll admit it, Lord—I don't like people messing with my family. When bullies start picking on my brother or sister, I get mad. And when my mom is crying because someone hurt her feelings, I just want to come out swinging. I want to protect those I love. I know You understand how I feel. You're the best protector of all! You don't like people messing with Your kids. You love and defend us whenever we're in trouble. Help me not to lose my temper or do the wrong thing when I'm upset. I want to show love, even to those who pick on us, so that they can see Your light shining through my life. Help me, I pray. Amen.

Say to your brothers, "You are my people,"
and to your sisters, "You have received mercy."
HOSEA 2:1 ESV

PART OF A BIGGER FAMILY

Dear God, sometimes I like to think about my family—not just the people in my house, but my aunts, uncles, cousins, grandparents, and so on. I even like to imagine what my great-grandparents and their relatives must have been like. Do I look or act like any of them, Lord? I'm just curious. The truth is, I come from a super-huge family, one that goes back generations. Before I was even born, people in my family were praying for me. I can just imagine my great-grandmother praying for all of the children to come. Wow! I want to be like that, Lord. Even now, while I'm young, I lift up my future children, grandchildren, and great-grandchildren to You! I love being part of such a big, amazing family. May we all live to serve and love You. Amen.

And he took them the same hour of the night and washed their wounds; and he was baptized at once, he and all his family.
Acts 16:33 esv

⑊ A MIGHTY MAN OF GOD ⑊

You're a tough guy, and you want everyone to know it. But there's something more important than having muscles. . . you've got to have a strong spiritual life. It's time to build those spiritual muscles, kid! If you really want to be tough, then be tough in Christ.

MR. TOUGH GUY

I like to act like I'm tough, God, but sometimes I'm just pretending. Deep down, I get really scared. I don't know how to be powerful. I can't fix things on my own, no matter how hard I try. Then You remind me that true power comes from You, Lord. Without You, I'm sunk! With You, I'm a mighty guy of God, one who can speak to mountains and watch them move. So today I choose to find my strength in You, not myself. No more Mr. Tough Guy. I'll let You be the strong one. Whew! It's such a relief to know I don't have to fix everything on my own. Amen.

⑊ ⑊ ⑊

All the days of Saul there was bitter war with the Philistines, and whenever Saul saw a mighty or brave man, he took him into his service.
1 SAMUEL 14:52 NIV

HELLO, GOD. ARE YOU THERE?

Okay, I have to admit something, Lord. Sometimes I wonder if You're really there. I pray to You and I don't know if You hear me. I feel like my prayers are bouncing off the ceiling. Sometimes it even feels a little weird to pray to Someone I can't see with my own eyes. But that's when I need to trust. I need to believe even when I can't see or feel Your presence. Your Word says You'll never leave me or forsake me. That means You're always with me even when it doesn't feel like it. Give me the faith and courage to believe even during those times, Lord. You're right there! Amen.

"Be strong and courageous. Do not fear or be in dread of them, for it is the Lord your God who goes with you. He will not leave you or forsake you."
Deuteronomy 31:6 esv

PUTTING GOD FIRST

Sometimes I forget that I should be putting You first, God. Your name should be the first name I speak when I wake up in the morning. Your thoughts and opinions should be the ones that matter most to me. I spend so much time worrying what other people think about me when I should be focused more on what You think. When I put You first in my life, every-thing else falls into place. Everything comes into order. Today I choose to make my relationship with You the most important thing. I can't wait to see how everything comes together. Amen.

"But seek first the kingdom of God and his righteousness, and all these things will be added to you."
MATTHEW 6:33 ESV

GOD'S WORD

The Bible is so awesome, Lord! It's filled with so many cool stories from Bible times: Joseph and his amazing coat of many colors. Noah, a man of courage who followed Your orders, even though they didn't make sense at the time. Samson, a man of strength. David, a man who loved You with his whole heart. Mary, a young woman who became the mother of Jesus. The disciples, who chose to follow Jesus no matter what. I can learn so many lessons from these stories! They teach me how to be brave, how to stand up to my enemies, and how to love and serve You more. I'm so grateful for the Word of God! Thanks for sharing it with us, Lord. What a blessing! Amen.

For the word of God is alive and active. Sharper than any double-edged sword, it penetrates even to dividing soul and spirit, joints and marrow; it judges the thoughts and attitudes of the heart.
HEBREWS 4:12 NIV

PRAYER TIME

I love hanging out with You, Lord. I know I can tell You anything—the things I'm worried about, the things I love, even the things I'm hoping to do with my life. You're the best listener ever! Mostly, I love telling You how great You are. You're awesome, God! There's something so great about praising You. I could sing a song right now just to celebrate Your goodness! Thanks for always being there, Lord. Thanks for keeping Your door open and Your light on so that I can come any time of the day or night and tell You what I'm going through. I'm so grateful for the time we spend together. I love You, Lord! Amen.

Don't worry about anything; instead, pray about everything. Tell God what you need, and thank him for all he has done. Then you will experience God's peace, which exceeds anything we can understand. His peace will guard your hearts and minds as you live in Christ Jesus.
PHILIPPIANS 4:6–7 NLT

WORSHIP

I haven't really understood this word *worship*, Lord. Sometimes I think it's part of our church service, when we sing songs. Other times I think it's when we pray or say words like, "I love You, Lord! I adore You!" Sometimes I think worship is how we live our lives as believers. So I read Your Word, and I see that it's all of the above! True worship is living a life that is totally devoted to You, Jesus. When I put You first, the songs I sing, the prayers I pray, the words of devotion I speak, the way I talk to others, the way I dress, the people I hang out with. . .all of those things become an act of worship. Today I choose to be completely devoted! May my whole life be an act of worship, Lord. Amen.

Oh come, let us worship and bow down;
let us kneel before the Lord, our Maker!
PSALM 95:6 ESV

GOD'S WAYS ARE HIGHER

I always think I know the best way to do things, Lord. I can be a real know-it-all sometimes. But I'm figuring out that You know best. When I don't get my way and feel like complaining, You whisper, "I've got something better!" in my ear. Today I choose to trust You even when things don't seem to be working out. Even when my friend won't speak to me. Even when my prayers aren't answered the way I think they should be. Even when the bullies are doing their thing. I'll trust in You because I know You've got bigger, better things coming. I can't wait to see what You have in store for me, Lord. Amen.

Now to him who is able to do immeasurably more than all we ask or imagine, according to his power that is at work within us, to him be glory in the church and in Christ Jesus throughout all generations, for ever and ever! Amen.
EPHESIANS 3:20–21 NIV

FAITH

I want to talk to You about this word *faith*, Lord. Dad says I need to have it, even when I can't see proof with my own eyes. Here's an example: When my grandpa got sick and had to go in the hospital, it looked like he wouldn't make it. So I prayed. At first it didn't look like he was getting better, but then I really, truly started to believe in my heart that You could heal him if You wanted to. And Grandpa got well because it was Your will, Lord. You healed him. Show me how to believe, even when it feels impossible, Lord. I want to be a kid who has great faith in You. Amen.

Since we have been made right with God by our faith, we have peace with God. This happened through our Lord Jesus Christ, who through our faith has brought us into that blessing of God's grace that we now enjoy. And we are happy because of the hope we have of sharing God's glory.
ROMANS 5:1–2 NCV

THE VOICE OF THE HOLY SPIRIT

I can hear Your voice, Lord! Through Your Spirit, You speak to my heart. You whisper words that change everything. You say things like, "Peace, be still!" when I'm angry. You make the knots in my stomach go away when You say words like, "Calm down, kid. It's going to be okay." I don't know if I'll ever hear Your voice with my ears, but for now, go on speaking to my heart. I need Your wisdom and Your guidance, especially when I'm at school or hanging out with my friends. I want to be a boy who knows Your voice, one who listens and then obeys. I'll grow big and strong as long as I keep listening, Lord. Amen.

As He spoke to me the Spirit entered me and set me on my feet; and I heard Him speaking to me.
EZEKIEL 2:2 NASB

THE KING'S SON

I get it, Lord! I'm a son of the King! Because I'm Your son, I'm royalty. I can almost picture my armor now! You chose me. You called me to live an amazing life as Your kid. You've set me apart to do great things for You. I want to live every single day as a kid you can be proud of, one with an excellent attitude. May I shine like a star for You, always doing or saying the things You would do or say. That's what a true prince does, after all. He's a reflection of his father, the King. Thanks for inviting me to be Your son, Lord. Amen.

But you are a chosen race, a royal priesthood,
a holy nation, a people for his own possession,
that you may proclaim the excellencies of him who
called you out of darkness into his marvelous light.
1 PETER 2:9 ESV

⊪ TAKE OUT THE TRASH ⊪

There's stinky stuff in your life that needs to go. No, not just those dirty socks you shoved under the bed. Real stuff. Stuff that's holding you back from being all you can be. Time to take a look at it and then toss it all in the trash!

TEMPER, TEMPER!

I don't know where the anger comes from sometimes, Lord. I'm having a normal day, then—*bam!*—someone does something that sets me off like a rocket ship! Wow, do I know how to explode! I come out swinging and yelling, red in the face with anger. Oops. I don't mean to get angry. And I'm always embarrassed after it's over, especially when Mom or Dad or one of my teachers calls me out on it. Can You help me with my anger, Lord? I don't want to be known as the guy who blows up at people. I want to have a calm, steady spirit. . .a great attitude. Today I give You my anger and ask You to change my heart forever. Amen.

⊪ ⊪ ⊪ ⊪

"In your anger do not sin": Do not let the sun go down while you are still angry, and do not give the devil a foothold.
EPHESIANS 4:26–27 NIV

PRIDE

It's one thing to be proud of a football team, Lord. It's another thing to be so proud of yourself that you think you're better than everyone else. I see people do this all the time. They think they're better at sports or better at singing—stuff like that. Or maybe they think they're better because of the color of their skin or where they go to school. People get prideful about a lot of things. Only You can erase pride, Lord. Only You can tell people that they need to treat others the way they want to be treated. Start right here, right now, I pray. If there is any pride inside of me, I ask You to wipe it away, Lord. Toss it in the trash! I want to care more about others than myself. Amen.

Don't be jealous or proud, but be humble and consider others more important than yourselves. Care about them as much as you care about yourselves and think the same way that Christ Jesus thought.
PHILIPPIANS 2:3–5 CEV

HYPOCRISY

I'll admit it, Lord—I'm not always who I say I am. I tell others that I'm a Christian, that I follow You, and then I treat them badly. I get angry. I throw a fit. I want to have my own way. I bend to peer pressure and follow the crowd. In other words, I'm a hypocrite. That's not very Christlike, I know. Today, please help me be exactly who I say I am. I want to toss hypocrisy in the trash! Show me how to treat others fairly, with the kind of love You would show them. I want to be a reflection of You, Jesus, so help me to do what You would do and to say what You would say. Amen.

*"Nothing is covered up that will not be revealed,
or hidden that will not be known."*
LUKE 12:2 ESV

BROKEN PROMISES

I know You never break Your promises, Lord. If You said it, You'll do it. Me? I break promises all the time. Oh, I don't mean to, but I do. I tell Mom I'm going to clean my room, then I don't follow through. I tell my kid brother I'll hang out with him, but end up spending time with my friends instead. I promise my dad that I'll do better at guarding my temper, then I slip up and yell at my brother again. Yep, I'm ashamed to admit it, but sometimes I'm a promise-breaker, not a promise-keeper. But with Your help I can do better. I can toss those broken promises into the trash and then do what I said I'd do. Thanks for helping me with this, Lord! Amen.

In view of all this, make every effort to respond to God's promises. Supplement your faith with a generous provision of moral excellence, and moral excellence with knowledge.
2 PETER 1:5 NLT

ATTITUDE CHECK!

I don't always have the best attitude, Lord. Some days I'm just in a bad mood. I don't really know why. Maybe because I'm tired or because of stuff going on at school. I'm sorry about my bad attitude. Help me to be a kid who's positive and up-beat. When others look at me, I don't want them to say, "Wow, he's cranky!" Just the opposite! I want them to look at me and say, "I want to be like him. He always has a smile on his face." That can only happen if I stick close to You. You're the ultimate teacher when it comes to great attitudes. So today I choose to be like You. Please help me, Lord. Amen.

Throw off your old sinful nature and your former way of life. . . . Instead, let the Spirit renew your thoughts and attitudes.
EPHESIANS 4:22–23 NLT

APATHY

Lord, I didn't really understand this word *apathy* until recently. When I'm apathetic, I just don't care. I don't care if my room is a mess. I don't care if I get my homework done. I don't care if I get in trouble at school. I don't care if I hurt my sister's feelings. I'm just kind of "blah" about everything. But now I understand that You care about all of these things. And I already know my parents care! I hear about it. . . a lot. I need to toss my apathy aside and start caring again! Would You help me with that, Lord? The only way I'll ever truly care is if You show me how. If it matters to You, from now on it's going to matter to me. Amen.

"So, because you are lukewarm, and neither hot nor cold, I will spit you out of my mouth."
REVELATION 3:16 ESV

LACK OF SELF-CONTROL

Self-control is hard, Lord! "Look, but don't touch!" "Stay away from the candy jar!" "Don't disobey!" So many times I just want to dive in and get what I want, even when it's not good for me. But You are teaching me self-control. You're showing me that it's healthier to control my urges. The next time I don't get what I want, I won't throw a fit. I'll just submit to Your will, Father. You know what's best. You're always looking out for me, and I'm so grateful for that! Teach me how to control myself, please. I know I'll be better off in the long run. Amen.

But the fruit of the Spirit is love, joy, peace, forbearance, kindness, goodness, faithfulness, gentleness and self-control. Against such things there is no law.
GALATIANS 5:22–23 NIV

GOSSIP

Here's something I really need to toss in the trash, Lord: gossip! It's a terrible thing. I know what it's like to be the kid everyone else is talking about. It hurts. . .a lot. I also know what it's like to talk about others. I don't really do it on purpose, but sometimes I get caught up in conversations and before you know it—*bam!*—I'm gossiping. I don't want to be like this. Would You help me, please? Next time I start to gossip, put a clamp on my tongue. Stop me from saying bad things. Don't let me join in—laughing at someone behind his back just because he's different or made a mistake. I want to be a good example for others, Lord, but I need Your help tossing this one overboard! Amen.

Don't let anyone trick you with foolish talk. God punishes everyone who disobeys him and says foolish things. So don't have anything to do with anyone like that.
Ephesians 5:6–7 CEV

THE WORDS I SAY

Lord, it's not easy to hold my tongue. So many times, I want to get things off my chest, to speak my mind. I want my voice to be heard. Sometimes it doesn't feel fair that I don't have a chance to talk when I want to. I'm learning, though, that most times it's better to guard my tongue, not to lash out when I'm angry or anxious. It's tough, keeping my mouth closed! I'm so tempted to say the wrong thing or to speak in anger! I have to work extra-hard not to say things I want to say. But with Your help I can control myself. I can toss those words in the trash. Instead of telling others, I'll tell you, Jesus. You're the best one to solve these problems, anyway. Thanks for Your help with this, Lord. Amen.

Do not be quick with your mouth, do not be hasty in your heart to utter anything before God. God is in heaven and you are on earth, so let your words be few.
ECCLESIASTES 5:2 NIV

WHAT A MESS!

I'll admit it, Lord—it's hard for me to keep things clean sometimes. I shove my dirty clothes under the bed. I let things stack up in my closet. I forget to take out the trash. There's dust all over my dresser. I don't make my bed. Sometimes I just forget, but other times I think, *Who cares?* Then I remember that You care. You're training me to be a good soldier in Your army, one who takes good care of his stuff. So I'll start the cleanup process now, Lord. It's going to be a tough job because there's so much to do, but I'll give it my best shot. No more messes in my future! I'm tossing them in the trash. Amen.

If we confess our sins, he is faithful and just to forgive us our sins and to cleanse us from all unrighteousness.
1 JOHN 1:9 ESV

⑾ UNDER CONSTRUCTION ⑾

You are a work in progress, kiddo. You're not perfect, but you're doing the best you can to be like Jesus, and that's a good thing. Sure, you'll make mistakes. We all do. But keep on keeping on! You're headed in the right direction.

BOY UNDER CONSTRUCTION

Sometimes I feel like I'm under construction, Lord. I wonder if I'll ever be finished. Just about the time I think I'm doing okay, like I've made progress, I do something to mess up. Talk about being disappointed in myself! Then it's back to the starting line for me. I don't let it hold me back though. I know I have plenty of time to grow and change, but I'm definitely going to need Your help. Go ahead and fix the areas of my life that need fixing, even if it's not easy on me. I want to be the best I can possibly be when I get older. Thanks for taking the time to shape me into Your image, Lord. Amen.

But as for you, continue in what you have learned and have firmly believed, knowing from whom you learned it and how from childhood you have been acquainted with the sacred writings, which are able to make you wise for salvation through faith in Christ Jesus.
2 TIMOTHY 3:14–15 ESV

LET'S START OVER

I need a do-over, Lord. I really messed this one up. I said something—or did something—I wish I could take back. Can I just begin again? I'm so glad the Bible says I can! *Whew!* I don't know where I'd be if You didn't give second chances. Show me the right steps to take to make things right whenever I mess up, Lord. Teach me to come to You and ask forgiveness then make things right with the people I've hurt. I want to honor You, Lord, so show me how to turn things around in a hurry when I've made mistakes. I know I'm not the only one who messes up, but I want to be quick to fix things. . . with Your help. Amen.

Do not let any unwholesome talk come out of your mouths, but only what is helpful for building others up according to their needs, that it may benefit those who listen.
EPHESIANS 4:29 NIV

SPIRITUAL GROWTH

My body is growing and changing so much, Lord! I'm definitely under construction! Sometimes I look at pictures from a year or two ago, and I hardly recognize the kid staring back at me. He looks totally different now. But I'm not just changing on the outside. I'm changing on the inside too, Lord. As I read my Bible and pray, I'm growing, growing, growing on the inside. I'm becoming a stronger Christian. My faith is growing. It's not always easy, but I'm learning so much. I trust You to "grow me" into the man of God You want me to be. This is going to be a better adventure than any movie I've ever watched! Amen.

Finally, let the mighty strength of the Lord make you strong. Put on all the armor that God gives, so you can defend yourself against the devil's tricks.
EPHESIANS 6:10–11 CEV

FINISH WHAT YOU START

It's not always easy to finish what I start, Lord. I'm terrific at starting—art projects, school assignments, cleaning my room, and so on. But sometimes I get bored and don't feel like finishing. I give up before the job is done. How come I have so much energy when I start, but I give up so quickly? Do I get bored, or what? I need Your help to finish, Father! I want to be known as someone who finishes well. It's pointless to start well and fizzle out, after all! So give me strength to get the job done, Lord. . .the whole job. I'll definitely need Your help with this. Amen.

I press on to reach the end of the race and receive the heavenly prize for which God, through Christ Jesus, is calling us.
PHILIPPIANS 3:14 NLT

PATIENCE

I'm not very patient, Lord. When I want something, I want it now! Who wants to wait until Christmas to get the latest, greatest video game or bike? I'm definitely a work in progress, Lord! Sometimes I forget that waiting can be a good thing. You are teaching me to be patient, though, so I have to try. It wouldn't be good for me to get everything I wanted right away, anyway. I wouldn't appreciate things as much. I'd be spoiled. So I'll wait as patiently as I can for the things I hope to get one day. And while I'm waiting, I'll go ahead and thank You for all of the things You've already blessed me with. What an amazing Father You are! Amen.

But if we hope for what we do not see,
we wait for it with patience.
ROMANS 8:25 ESV

HUMILITY

Lord, sometimes I forget to be humble. I get a little puffed up. My attitude kicks in. I brag about myself. I tell other people about all the cool stuff I've done—my good grades, my talents, my abilities. I show off. Oh, I'm not bragging on purpose. Sometimes I just forget that singing my own praises isn't the best way to get people to like me. Will You help me with this? Whenever I'm tempted to brag, remind me that all of my abilities come from You. They're not my own doing. If I'm going to brag on anyone, let me brag on You, Jesus! You're the best, after all. Amen.

*Be completely humble and gentle;
be patient, bearing with one another in love.*
EPHESIANS 4:2 NIV

ADDICTIONS

It's hard to admit, Lord, but I'm kind of addicted to a few things. Take video games, for instance. I like to play them. . . and play them. . .and play them. I'm also a little addicted to certain Netflix shows. And certain foods—I like candy and junk food a lot. But I don't want to be addicted. I want to be able to stop playing a game when Mom says, "Time's up!" or to toss the junk food in the trash. But a part of me still wants to keep doing what I'm doing. Man, I could use some construction in this part of my life. I'm so glad You're not going to give up on me, Lord! Whew! Amen.

No temptation has overtaken you that is not common to man. God is faithful, and he will not let you be tempted beyond your ability, but with the temptation he will also provide the way of escape, that you may be able to endure it.
1 CORINTHIANS 10:13 ESV

BOUNDARIES

I didn't really understand the word *boundaries* when I was little, Lord. Now I get it! There are boundaries—rules and limits—to keep me safe. When I cross those boundaries, dangerous things can happen. So I choose to live within the boundaries You've given me in Your Word. I'll obey my parents, love others, and respect the people You've placed in authority in my life—my parents, grandparents, teachers, police officers, church leaders, and so on. I'll obey the law and follow the rules because I know my life will be blessed when I do. Thanks for boundaries, Lord. I'm so glad You keep me safe and sound. Amen.

Let your foot be seldom in your neighbor's house,
lest he have his fill of you and hate you.
PROVERBS 25:17 ESV

THOSE THINGS I SAID

Lord, I said some things I shouldn't have. I hurt someone's feelings. Now I feel like a goober. I shouldn't have done it, but sometimes my anger gets the best of me. It's too late to take things back, but I've done my best. I said I'm sorry. I asked for forgiveness—from the person and from You. I know I'm not perfect, but I sure wish I didn't struggle so much with mistakes. I know You want to change my heart so that I'm more careful next time. I'm okay with that. In fact, I'm glad You're changing me. I guess it's going to take a while, but I will do my best to be patient. At least I'm moving in the right direction. Thanks for giving me extra chances, Lord. Amen.

*Let no corrupting talk come out of your mouths,
but only such as is good for building up, as fits the
occasion, that it may give grace to those who hear.*
EPHESIANS 4:29 ESV

FAITHFUL IN THE LITTLE THINGS

I'm always asking You to use me in big ways, Lord. I want to do great things for You! But sometimes I forget that You're testing me in the little tasks before giving me big stuff to do. You're watching to see how I do with things like keeping my room clean or staying on top of homework or treating my siblings in a loving way. I want to pass the test! I want You to know that You can trust me to make a real difference in people's lives one day. Show me how to be faithful in the little things, Lord, so that one day great big opportunities will come my way. Amen.

"One who is faithful in a very little is also faithful in much, and one who is dishonest in a very little is also dishonest in much."
LUKE 16:10 ESV

⏸ IN THE GAME ⏸

You're in the game, and you're in it to win it. Whether you like to admit it or not, sometimes you're a little competitive. Of course, God is more interested in matters of the heart than in who wins the big game. Does that mean you shouldn't give it your best shot? Of course not! Play the game and give it your best, but never forget that you're always a winner in God's sight.

ATHLETICS

Father, everywhere I turn there are sports! Baseball. Soccer. Basketball. Football. Wrestling. Whew! I could try so many different things! Today I want to thank You for athletics, Lord. It's a great way to stay healthy and have fun at the same time. And when I'm on a sports team, I have lots of new friends. We do fun things together—on the field and off. Help me choose wisely, Lord. Will I be a ballplayer? A runner? An Olympic swimmer? Will I stick with it for years or just try it out for a while? I don't really know at this point, but I'm having fun figuring it out! Thanks for all of the opportunities, and thanks for my amazing friends. Amen.

⏸ ⏸ ⏸ ⏸

An athlete is not crowned unless he competes according to the rules.
2 TIMOTHY 2:5 ESV

GOOD SPORTSMANSHIP

I hear people say, "Be a good sport," all the time, Lord. I haven't really stopped to think about what that means until now. I guess being a good sport means I'm okay if the other team wins. It means I have a good attitude, even if I don't like the referee's call. It means I'm going to shake my opponent's hand and wish him a good game, even when I hope my team takes the prize. Life gives me plenty of opportunities to be a good sport—on the field and off. My attitude is important no matter where I go. I'll do my best to have great sportsmanship, Lord. Amen.

Do not rejoice when your enemy falls, and let not your heart be glad when he stumbles, lest the LORD see it and be displeased, and turn away his anger from him.
PROVERBS 24:17–18 ESV

IT'S HOW YOU PLAY THE GAME

I know You've been watching, Lord. I start off playing the game so well; then something goes wrong. I get frustrated. I kick the dirt with my shoes. I mumble under my breath. I give up. I complain and point fingers at others, blaming them for my bad day. I know my behavior is wrong, so please forgive me. Give me an attitude adjustment. When I'm upset like that—whether I'm on the field or at school—I ask You to take over. Give me good thoughts. Help me to persevere and not quit. If I'm having a bad day, I don't want to blame it on others. That does no good. Instead, I'll choose to believe that things will get better as long as I keep my head in the game.

An athlete is not crowned unless he
competes according to the rules.
2 TIMOTHY 2:5 ESV

A THREE-POINT SHOT

Some days are awesome, Lord! It's like everything I touch turns to gold. I could knock a ball out of the stadium or land a three-point shot. That's how perfect everything is. Everyone cheers me on. They clap and holler, "Woo-hoo! You're a superstar!" I'm not sure why some days are like that and others are so, well, *awful*. I wish every day could be a three-point-shot day. When things are going well—during the game or at school or at home—I don't want to be a bragger. It's okay if other people say nice things about my performance, but I really don't want to be the kind of person who brags on himself. Will You help me with that? Thanks, Lord! Amen.

Let another praise you, and not your own mouth; a stranger, and not your own lips.
PROVERBS 27:2 ESV

STRIKING OUT

Lord, some days I try so hard—at school, with friends, on the field—and absolutely nothing seems to go right. No matter how many times I shoot the basketball, I can't get it through the hoop. No matter how many times I swing my bat at the baseball, I strike out. Why, Lord? I've practiced so hard, and I know I can do it. Why are some days so stinking awful? On those days, remind me of what's really important. Winning and losing shouldn't be the main thing. I want to stay focused on You, not on myself. I give my bad days back to You, Lord— not so that You can turn me into a winner, but because I know You understand what it's like to have a rough day. I've read Your Word, and I know You had some rough days too.

For while bodily training is of some value, godliness is of value in every way, as it holds promise for the present life and also for the life to come.
1 TIMOTHY 4:8 ESV

TUG-OF-WAR

Sometimes my friendships are like a game of tug-of-war, Lord. This friend pulls me one direction, and that friend pulls me in another direction. Everyone wants me on their team, but they're not being good sports about it. In fact, they're being demanding and rude. I feel like I'm stuck in the middle, and I really don't know what to do. Show me how to be a friend to everyone and not play favorites. I'm tired of getting pushed and pulled around. I want to be a shining example of You, Lord, so give me Your rules for the game and I'll play to win. Amen.

Every athlete exercises self-control in all things. They do it to receive a perishable wreath, but we an imperishable.
1 CORINTHIANS 9:25 ESV

EXERCISE

I want to stay in good shape, Lord, and I know that means I need to exercise more. Can You give me ideas? I want to do things that will be fun—playing sports, swimming, playing games with my friends. And while I'm working on my physical body, help me to exercise my mind too. I want to stay alert and active so that the enemy doesn't tempt me to do the wrong things. May I be strong in body, mind, and soul, Father. That way I can be all You've created me to be. Amen.

For while bodily training is of some value,
godliness is of value in every way, as it holds promise
for the present life and also for the life to come.
1 TIMOTHY 4:8 ESV

TEAMWORK

Lord, I love hanging out with the team after a game. We go out to eat together. Everyone laughs and talks and has a great time. Doesn't matter if we won the game or lost—as long as we're together, we're having a blast. Sometimes we get a little loud and crazy in restaurants, but we're working on that! I've heard people say there's power in numbers, and that's how I feel when I'm with my friends and team members. I feel like we're a powerful force, an amazing group of guys. Together, we are invincible! Thanks for teamwork, Lord. Amen.

*I appeal to you, brothers, by the name of our Lord
Jesus Christ, that all of you agree, and that there
be no divisions among you, but that you be united
in the same mind and the same judgment.*
1 CORINTHIANS 1:10 ESV

VICTORY

I love to win, Lord! I think everyone does. It's great when my sports team wins or when I come in first in a school competition. But I'm learning that the best victory of all—far better than getting an A+ on a paper—is trusting in You. When I place my trust in You, even in the hard times, You always lead me to victory. When I'm feeling sick, You make me whole. When my heart is hurting, You bring peace and comfort. When I'm scared, You make me bold. I could never achieve these things on my own, Lord. I need You so much. With my hand in Yours, I'll always be victorious! Amen.

But thanks be to God! He gives us the victory through our Lord Jesus Christ.
1 CORINTHIANS 15:57 NIV

RUN THE RACE

I'm not sure I'll make it to the finish line, Lord! My legs are quivering like a bowl of pudding. I'm out of breath. The other runners are way ahead of me. I'm lagging behind, ready to give up. Then I remember that Your Word says I should run my race and not give up. I think about Jesus—how He made it all the way to the finish line—the cross—and gave His life for mine. On days when I feel like I can't go on, I want to remember His sacrifice. If He could do that for me, then surely I can keep going even though I feel like quitting. No quitters here, Lord! Amen.

Do you not know that in a race all the runners run, but only one receives the prize? So run that you may obtain it.
1 CORINTHIANS 9:24 ESV

⊪ A TRUE GENTLEMAN ⊪

You've heard it so many times: "Act like a gentleman." What does that mean, though? Does it mean you should open the door for ladies or sit quietly while others do all the talking? Does it mean you let others have a turn first and wait until the end? This whole "gentleman" thing can be kind of confusing. Time to figure it out!

OTHERS FIRST

Lord, I'm still a kid. You already know that. Because I'm still a kid, I don't always remember stuff I've been told, like "Put others first." People are always saying that. I guess I should think more highly of others than myself. That's part of what being a gentleman is all about—paying attention to the needs of others and doing my best to help when I can. I'm going to need Your help with this, Lord. I don't always remember to think of others first. Sometimes I just want what I want when I want it. I'm sorry about that. But I do want to be a gentleman, so please show me how. Amen.

⊪ ⊪ ⊪ ⊪

"Every healthy tree bears good fruit, but the diseased
tree bears bad fruit. A healthy tree cannot bear bad fruit,
nor can a diseased tree bear good fruit. Every tree that does
not bear good fruit is cut down and thrown into the fire."
MATTHEW 7:17–19 ESV

SHE'S A LADY

Lord, I'm doing my best to treat girls differently than boys. It's not always easy, especially with those girls who act like tomboys! Man, they're tough! But I know You want me to treat girls with respect and kindness. One day I'll be all grown-up and those girls will have become ladies. I'll do my best to speak kindly to them, not just then, but now. And I'll open doors for them too and make sure no one picks on them. That's what a gentleman does. And while I'm at it, I'll treat my mom, my grandma, and the other ladies in my life with the respect they deserve too. Show me how, I pray. Amen.

"I will raise up for them a prophet like you from among their brothers. And I will put my words in his mouth, and he shall speak to them all that I command him."
DEUTERONOMY 18:18 ESV

STOP AND THINK

It happens all the time, Lord. I'm so busy going here and there that I sometimes plow ahead of people in line. Would You help me stop and think before I insist on being first in line? I don't want people to think I'm pushy or rude. And would You help me with something else too? Sometimes I interrupt people when they're talking. I don't do it on purpose—I'm just not paying attention, is all. So help me pay attention, please. This one's going to take a lot of work, but I can do it with Your help. Thanks, Lord. Amen.

Do nothing from selfish ambition or conceit, but in humility count others more significant than yourselves.
PHILIPPIANS 2:3 ESV

DISAGREEMENTS

I don't like to disagree with people, Lord, but it happens. I get into an argument with my sister. I fight with my best friend. I even get mad at my mom. I know, I know! That's not very gentlemanly of me! When I disagree, it means I'm out of agreement with that person. Being out of agreement with someone is tough, no matter who it is. But You can solve all problems, Lord. You can mend our disagreements and help us stay close. No, I won't always agree with others. But that doesn't mean we can't be friends. With Your help, my relationships with others can grow stronger in spite of our differences. Thanks for showing me that. Amen.

Be brave when you face your enemies. Your courage will show them that they are going to be destroyed, and it will show you that you will be saved. God will make all of this happen.
PHILIPPIANS 1:28 CEV

FORGIVENESS

Ugh! Sometimes I get really mad when people hurt my feelings or say bad things about me, Lord. I don't want to forgive them. I wonder why I should have to. They're the ones who were in the wrong, after all. But Your Word says I need to forgive, even when it's really, really hard. It's not just biblical; it's the gentlemanly thing to do. So today I ask for Your help. I can't forgive unless You give me the power to do so. Help me to forgive those who've hurt me and then let go of any pain or bitterness. I want to walk in freedom, Lord, so show me how to release those who've wronged me. Heal those relationships, I pray, and teach me how to live in love. Amen.

Make allowance for each other's faults, and forgive anyone who offends you. Remember, the Lord forgave you, so you must forgive others.
COLOSSIANS 3:13 NLT

KINDNESS

I love when people are kind to me, Lord! It makes my day when they go out of their way to treat me well. Sometimes all it takes is a smile or a nod. Funny how a bad mood can change in a hurry when someone shows kindness! I want to be that sort of friend to others. May I be known for my kindness. When others look at me, I want them to say, "Oh, I know him. He's a real gentleman, someone who always treats everyone well." Show me today how I can bless someone else with a kind deed. Make it creative, Lord! I want to bring a smile to a friend or loved one's face. Would You help me come up with a fun idea, Lord? I know it's going to be great. Amen.

Love never hurts a neighbor,
so loving is obeying all the law.
ROMANS 13:10 NCV

A FRIEND TO THE FRIENDLESS

I don't always feel like I have a lot of friends, Lord. And sometimes I wonder if the guys who pretend to be my friends really are. Sometimes their actions don't line up with their words! I know what it's like to feel left out, which is why I feel sad when I see other kids being deliberately left out. They don't get picked to be in the group because they're different. It's not right, Lord. No one should be excluded. . .for any reason. Today, give me the courage to be the sort of person who goes out of his way to include everyone. I can do it with Your help, Lord. I know You love everyone just the same—and I want to love others that way too. Amen.

So let's stop condemning each other. Decide instead to live in such a way that you will not cause another believer to stumble and fall.
ROMANS 14:13 NLT

BOLDNESS

God, sometimes I feel a little shy. I see someone being hurt by others, and I don't say anything. I'm scared of what people will think. I want to speak up, but I don't have the courage. I'd rather hide in my room and keep to myself. It's easier than sharing what's on my mind. Help me become bolder, Father. Seriously! A real gentleman speaks up. He defends the defenseless. Give me the kind of power that only comes from You—superhero stuff! I don't want to be a fraidy-cat anymore. I want to stick up for what's right and help those who need a friend. That can only happen if I'm bold. I need Your help, Lord, so that I can help others. Amen.

"But you will receive power when the Holy Spirit comes on you; and you will be my witnesses in Jerusalem, and in all Judea and Samaria, and to the ends of the earth."
ACTS 1:8 NIV

REAL OR FAKE?

It's hard to tell if people are the real deal sometimes. I know You can see into their hearts, Lord. You know when they're faking it. But I only see the outside, and sometimes I fall for their tricks. I get drawn into situations, only to be hurt by the tricksters. Today, give me supernatural vision to see when people are up to no good so that I can avoid them. I want to be friendly to others, but I don't want to be hurt. So help me avoid the hurters. Give me wisdom to know how to respond when I see people faking it. Most of all, make me the real deal—someone who truly loves You and puts others first. A real gentleman is never a faker, Lord. Help me, I pray. Amen.

If anyone says, "I love God," and hates his brother,
he is a liar; for he who does not love his brother whom
he has seen cannot love God whom he has not seen.
1 JOHN 4:20 ESV

SERVING THOSE WITH DISABILITIES

Father, today I'm thinking about the kids I know who have disabilities. They're amazing, Lord! Some are in wheelchairs, but that doesn't stop them! They're super-brave. They do all sorts of activities, even if it's hard. Others have disabilities that can't be seen, but they do amazing things too. The truth is, there are no limits, no matter what we're facing in this life. As long as we stick close to You, we can accomplish anything. So show me how I can help those who are struggling, I pray. Give them courage. Give them friends. Meet every need. And may I always see them as You do—as Your perfect, amazing kids. Amen.

*This is my prayer for you: that your love
will grow more and more; that you will have
knowledge and understanding with your love.*
PHILIPPIANS 1:9 NCV

ᚎᚂᚃ HARD WORK ᚃᚂᚎ

Whew! You're tired. Between school, chores, sports, church, and other activities, you're ready for a nap. It's not time to give up yet! God has big things for you to do, and they're going to require hard work on your part. Are you ready for it? Let's go!

MY BEST

Sometimes I feel a little lazy, Lord. I don't want to get out of bed. I don't feel like cleaning my room. I don't want to go to school. It's more fun to just lie around and play video games or hang out with my friends. But I know that hard work is part of Your plan. You are the hardest worker of all! You made the whole world and everything in it. That must've been exhausting! I want to be like You, so I'll work hard too. Give me the energy to get the job done, no matter what. Dirty dishes? No problem! A messy closet? I'll clean it up! Hungry dog that needs to be fed? I'm on it! Whatever tasks I'm given, I'll do my best to work hard with a smile on my face. Thank You for the chance to be more like You, Father. Amen.

Do not be lazy but work hard,
serving the Lord with all your heart.
ROMANS 12:11 NCV

FINDING YOUR CALLING

I wonder what I'm going to be when I grow up, but You already know, God! I think about it all the time. Will I be a teacher? A police officer? A dad? A missionary? Will I travel around the world exploring all sorts of amazing places I've never seen before? Will I work on a computer in an office or in a laboratory as a scientist? Will I be a doctor, caring for sick people, or will I be a plumber, unclogging sinks and toilets? I know it's going to be a lot of work, but thinking about the future is exciting. I have so many creative ideas. Until I'm grown, I choose to trust in You, Lord. I submit myself to Your will for my life. I know You have great things in store for me, and I'm grateful! Amen.

*But the LORD said to me, "Do not say, 'I am too
young.' You must go to everyone I send you
to and say whatever I command you."*
JEREMIAH 1:7 NIV

THINGS TO DO

Whew! I've got so many things to do, Lord! My calendar is full to the brim with school stuff, sports, church activities, family get-togethers, and so much more. I've got family vacations, homework, pets to take care of. I've got a messy bedroom to clean and friends to hang out with. Sometimes I wonder how I'll keep it all in balance. But You'll show me. You have great things for me to do, and I know You'll help with the details. Most of all, show me how to keep things in the right order. Priorities, priorities! Make sure I deal with the most important stuff first, I pray. Amen.

What you decide on will be done,
and light will shine on your ways.
JOB 22:28 NIV

CLEANLINESS

Okay Father, it's confession time. I know you see into the messy spots—my closet, under my bed, the bathroom. You know when I let dirty clothes pile up or dust bunnies gather. You see when I leave dirty dishes in the sink or icky, sticky cups filled with juice. You know when I forget to brush my teeth or wash my hair. You want me to live a clean life—my body, my clothes, and my surroundings. But I need Your help, Father! Cleanliness doesn't come naturally to me. So give me a plan to keep my stuff clean and organized. Remind me when it's time to take a shower or floss my teeth. I don't want to be smelly—I want to be smiley! Time to clean up my act, Lord. Amen.

Wash yourselves; make yourselves clean; remove the evil of your deeds from before my eyes; cease to do evil.
Isaiah 1:16 esv

YOUR BEST SELF

I don't always give my best, Lord. Sometimes I do things halfheartedly. I don't put all of my energy into some things, especially things like cleaning my room or helping with the dishes or laundry. I just don't seem to care about those things as much. Help me to care, Lord. I want to give my all, no matter what I'm doing—in school, at church, at home, even when I'm alone in my bedroom. Show me how to take care of the things that matter, and help me to care more so that I can be my best possible self. I want to care like You care. Amen.

Do not be conformed to this world, but be transformed by the renewal of your mind, that by testing you may discern what is the will of God, what is good and acceptable and perfect.
ROMANS 12:2 ESV

LIVING YOUR FAITH

God, I don't always live my faith. I know You see when I mess up. I tell others I'm a Christian, but then I slip up. I lie. I gossip. I give in to peer pressure. Sometimes it's hard work to be who I say I am, but I want to try harder. I want to be a person who lives out his faith. I need Your help, Father. Teach me how to be consistent, no matter what I'm going through. Even when others make me angry, show me how to love. When they say mean things about me, help me to respond with kindness. Make me the strongest "me" I can be—someone who loves You and loves others with his whole heart. I praise You in advance for the work You're doing in my heart. Amen.

Above all else, you must live in a way that brings honor to the good news about Christ. Then, whether I visit you or not, I will hear that all of you think alike. I will know that you are working together and that you are struggling side by side to get others to believe the good news.
PHILIPPIANS 1:27 CEV

GOOD GRADES

I might not be like Einstein, Lord. I'm not a supersonic student, one who gets every answer right on the test. But I try my best! I want to get good marks in school, not just because my parents think it's important, but because I know good grades will help me get into a good college and eventually get a great job. I'll admit it—I need to pay more attention to my studies and less time playing. I need to focus on my homework and not on the TV or tablet or phone. In short, I need to buckle down. Help me do my very best work, Lord. I want to shine like an academic superstar, with Your help. Amen.

Make every effort to add to your faith goodness; and to goodness, knowledge.
2 PETER 1:5 NIV

PROBLEM-SOLVING

Father, You know I'm not great at fixing stuff—broken things or broken relationships. Problem-solving isn't my thing. Let's face it, sometimes I'm better at getting into trouble than getting out of it. But with Your help I can become a great problem-solver. You're the best at fixing things, even things that don't look fixable. Today I ask You to give me supernatural problem-solving skills. When I feel stuck, whisper in my ear, "Try this!" or "Try that!" I know with Your help I can get better at getting *out* of sticky situations rather than into them. Amen.

I pray that your love will keep on growing and that you will fully know and understand how to make the right choices. Then you will still be pure and innocent when Christ returns. And until that day, Jesus Christ will keep you busy doing good deeds that bring glory and praise to God.
PHILIPPIANS 1:9–11 CEV

SCHOOL WOES

Some school days are harder than others, Lord. Things go wrong. I get in trouble for talking too much, I forget to do my homework, or I get a bad grade on a test. I struggle to learn, I end up getting in an argument with a friend, or I don't know the answer when the teacher calls on me. How embarrassing! Those days stink! I wish every school day could be perfect, but I know that's not going to happen, so I ask You to give me Your peace and courage on the hard days. Most of all, show me how to be a reflection of You during the hours I'm at school. I want to shine like a star, even on bad days. Amen.

Don't get angry. Don't be upset;
it only leads to trouble.
PSALM 37:8 NCV

WHY IS IT HARDER FOR ME?

Lord, I just don't get it. Some of my friends are amazing at sports. They hit home runs all the time. Me? I can barely hit the ball, even on a good day. And some of my friends are amazing students. It's easy for them to make an A on the test or impress their parents with awesome grades on their report card. Me? I have to struggle to make a B. I don't know why my life seems so much harder than others, Lord, but I'm not going to give up. One day, when I'm older and have a great job, I'll be glad I gave it my all and kept trying. Thanks for helping me. Amen.

Fear not, for I am with you; be not dismayed,
for I am your God; I will strengthen you, I will help you,
I will uphold you with my righteous right hand.
ISAIAH 41:10 ESV

⑊ SALVATION IN JESUS ⑊

The most important prayer you will ever pray is the one where you ask Jesus to come and live inside your heart, to be the King of your life. Have you done that yet? If not, today's the perfect day. Ask Him to forgive you for your sins; then watch as He takes away all of your mess-ups and leaves you white as snow!

WHITER THAN SNOW

I've been trying to figure this out, God. I mess up so many times—and not just in small ways. I have big-time mess-ups. And yet the Bible says that I can be whiter than snow, that all my sins can be erased. Sometimes I try really, really hard not to mess up, but I don't have enough power to do it on my own. That's why I need You! I know I can't wash away my own sins. Only Jesus can do that. So I come to You, Lord—again and again—because You keep on giving second chances. You forgive me and wash me clean then say, "It's okay! Start over!" Thanks for making me white as snow, Lord. Amen.

⑊ ⑊ ⑊ ⑊

"Come now, let us reason together, says the LORD: though your sins are like scarlet, they shall be as white as snow; though they are red like crimson, they shall become like wool."
ISAIAH 1:18 ESV

JESUS, MY SAVIOR

You came to save me, Jesus! You left heaven, that awesome, perfect place, and came all the way to earth as a baby, so that You could live a sinless life and then die on the cross, just for me. If I was the only person on earth, You still would have come. That's so amazing! You didn't want to miss one minute with me, so You made sure I received Your free gift of salvation. Now I'll get to live in heaven with You—*forever*! You saved me from my sin, my selfishness, and my bad habits. What a wonderful Savior You are, Jesus. I'm so thankful that You changed my life. Amen.

Jesus said to him, "I am the way, and the truth, and the life. No one comes to the Father except through me."
JOHN 14:6 ESV

REPENTANCE

I don't always do the right thing, Lord. I guess I don't have to tell You that because You know it already. You see everything, even down into my heart. You know when I'm tempted to do the wrong thing. But You're a loving, gracious Father! You make me want to do right. So today I choose to turn away from the bad things I've done. I'll point myself in a different direction. Please forgive me for the things I've done that have hurt others. I know I've broken Your heart at times. I want to live a godly life filled with possibilities. So I repent and turn back to You, Father. Thanks for welcoming me back even after I've made mistakes. Amen.

The Lord is not slow to fulfill his promise as some count slowness, but is patient toward you, not wishing that any should perish, but that all should reach repentance.
2 PETER 3:9 ESV

THE WORDS IN RED

Lord, I love Your Word! The Bible is filled with great advice for how to live my life. I especially love the words in red, the words of Jesus. When I read the red words, I know they're extra powerful, because Jesus spoke them out loud to His disciples, His followers, and to me! It's crazy-cool to think that He knew I would one day be alive! I can almost hear His voice now, as I read the words. They leap off the page! He's telling me to live a life that is pleasing to Him, to walk close to Him always, and to love others the way I want to be loved. No matter how many books I read, there will never be words more important than the ones in red. I promise to keep them close to my heart. Amen.

Because, if you confess with your mouth that
Jesus is Lord and believe in your heart that God
raised him from the dead, you will be saved.
ROMANS 10:9 ESV

THE GREAT LOVE OF JESUS

Jesus, Your love is deeper than any ocean. It reaches all the way down to the bottom when I'm hurting. It's higher than any mountain. It shines like a beam from a lighthouse that can be seen for miles away. It's tougher than an athlete's muscles, and it's able to work miracles, touching even the hardest heart. Your love means everything to me, Lord. It picks me up when I'm down, encourages me when I'm depressed, and makes me want to sing a song of praise. Thank You for loving me even when I make mistakes. You're so kind to me, even when I mess up. From the bottom of my heart, I thank You for Your amazing love. Amen!

But God shows his great love for us in this way:
Christ died for us while we were still sinners.
ROMANS 5:8 NCV

JESUS FIRST

You know every answer to every question, Lord! When I put You first in my life—above my friends, sports, electronics, schoolwork, family—everything else always works out. I'm not saying I always get it right. Sometimes things get out of order. I forget to put You first. Things go wrong, and I wonder why. Instead of going to You, asking for Your help, I try to fix things myself. Sometimes I just get panicked and think everything is falling apart. Then I remember. . .everything works better when the Boss is in charge. So today I submit to You. I don't want to be the boss of my life. Take Your place at the top, Lord, and I know everything will work out exactly as You have planned. Amen.

Jesus said to him, "I am the way, and the truth, and the life. No one comes to the Father except through me."
John 14:6 esv

FOLLOWING JESUS

Sometimes I'm a follower, Lord. I see some guys in a group and I want to be part of it so I do what they do. I dress like they dress. I talk like they talk. I make fun of the ones they make fun of. You don't want me to follow after people. I know that. But You do want me to follow You. So today I choose to love as You love, to serve as You serve, to act as You act. I want to be a Jesus-follower all the way! I know that means I have to change a few things—like my attitude and my desire to be like others—but that's okay! I really do want to be like You, Jesus, so lead me wherever You want me to go! Amen.

Then [Jesus] said to the crowd, "If any of you wants to be my follower, you must give up your own way, take up your cross daily, and follow me. If you try to hang on to your life, you will lose it. But if you give up your life for my sake, you will save it."
LUKE 9:23–24 NLT

THE SHAME GAME

God, I feel so ashamed sometimes. I do something wrong in complete secret then feel ashamed of myself. So I confess and make things right again. I should feel better after getting my wrongdoing off my chest, but I still feel ashamed every time I think about it. I try not to think about it, but then I feel ashamed all over again. It's time for that shame to go, in Jesus' name! I know a little conviction is a good thing, but You always forgive me and wash away my shame. You don't want me to wallow in it. You want me to start over with a smile on my face, ready to do better next time. So thanks for taking away my shame, Lord. I'm so happy to be done with it. Amen.

But the Lord GOD helps me; therefore I have not been disgraced; therefore I have set my face like a flint, and I know that I shall not be put to shame.
ISAIAH 50:7 ESV

SALVATION

Lord, I'm finally figuring out what it means to be saved. Jesus left heaven and came to earth. He died on the cross and gave His life in place of mine. If I accept His free gift of salvation, I can live forever in heaven. Wow! What a swap! What a trade-off! My sinful life in exchange for Jesus' perfect life? Of course I'm saying yes to that! It would be silly *not* to! I can't wait to share the good news with others so they can receive Your salvation too. I can't wait to see all the people in heaven who have said yes to Jesus. How fun that will be! Thanks for saving me, Lord. Amen.

For the wages of sin is death, but the free gift of God is eternal life in Christ Jesus our Lord.
ROMANS 6:23 ESV

JESUS

I hear people talking about Your Son, Jesus, all the time, Lord. Some people say He was a great man. Other people say He was a prophet. But I love what Your Word says: He was—and is—Your Son, and He did something no one else has ever done. He came to earth, knowing He would have to die on a cross. He chose to give up His life so that others could live. Who does that? Jesus lived an amazing, sinless life. He healed people and taught them how to live. There will never be anyone else like Jesus. Today I choose to praise Him at the top of my lungs! Amen.

For God so loved the world that he gave his one and only Son, that whoever believes in him shall not perish but have eternal life.
JOHN 3:16 NIV

⁍ GROWING UP ⁌

First you want it to happen fast; then you want it to slow down. Growing up ain't for sissies! There are so many changes going on in your heart, your mind, and your body. But don't worry. God already knows where these changes will lead you. It's going to be so much fun to watch it all happen!

CHANGES

Every day I look in the mirror and see changes, Lord! I'm growing. My parents keep having to buy me new clothes! Even my feet are changing. I've gone through a lot of socks and sneakers since I was a little kid. I know growing up is part of Your plan for me. Sometimes I like to imagine what I'll look like when I'm a teenager or a grown-up. Will I have my dad's hair? Will I have his big feet? Will I be short, tall, skinny, chubby? It's hard to know, but I'm excited to find out. So I've decided to enjoy the changes, Lord. Thanks for showing me the reflection in the mirror. It's fun to watch myself grow up! Amen.

And now, just as you accepted Christ Jesus as your Lord, you must continue to follow him. Let your roots grow down into him, and let your lives be built on him. Then your faith will grow strong in the truth you were taught, and you will overflow with thankfulness.
COLOSSIANS 2:6–7 NLT

ENJOYING CHILDHOOD

It's great to be a kid, Father! I don't have to worry about paying bills or having a job. Sure, I have to go to school, but that's kind of fun anyway. Being a kid means I get to play with friends, go swimming at the pool, learn cool new stuff, discover my talents, and spend lots of time with my family. I'm not in a big hurry to be a teenager, Lord. It's kind of cool to be young and carefree, to not have to worry about stuff like money problems or dating. I know things will change as I get older, but for now I plan to just go on being a kid and enjoying life. Amen.

Don't let anyone look down on you because you are young, but set an example for the believers in speech, in conduct, in love, in faith and in purity.
1 Timothy 4:12 niv

CRUSHES

A lot of the guys are doing it, Lord. . .they're talking about which girls they like, who's the prettiest, and that sort of thing. They have crushes on this one or that one. They talk about how cute the girl with blond hair is or how sweet and funny the one with dark hair is. I try not to get caught up in those conversations, Lord, but it's hard. Before long, I find myself talking about girls too. I know I'm too young for that, so help me. Guard my thoughts. Keep me pure. When the time is right, You'll show me. Until then, protect my heart, I pray. Amen.

Walk with the wise and become wise,
for a companion of fools suffers harm.
PROVERBS 13:20 NIV

PUBERTY

Lord, can I talk to You about something kind of awkward? I want to ask a few questions about puberty. My body is going through changes—and some of them are kind of weird—but I know that You designed my body, so I figure You're the best one to talk to about this. Am I going to change. . .a lot? Is it going to hurt? Will I feel strange? Are other boys going through the same changes? I know the Bible says You'll be with me every step of the way, so I choose to trust in You, no matter how much things change. You knew this was coming, Lord, and You even know what I'm going to look like on the other side of it. I wish I knew, but I guess I'll see soon enough. Help me through this transition, please! Amen.

Therefore we do not lose heart. Though outwardly we are wasting away, yet inwardly we are being renewed day by day. For our light and momentary troubles are achieving for us an eternal glory that far outweighs them all. So we fix our eyes not on what is seen, but on what is unseen, since what is seen is temporary, but what is unseen is eternal.
2 CORINTHIANS 4:16–18 NIV

A CHANGING VOICE

I know it's coming, God. My voice is going to change. Instead of being high-pitched or squeaky, it's going to get lower. Deeper. I'm not sure how or why this happens, but it's kind of cool. Instead of sounding like a boy, I'll sound like a man. Does this mean my singing voice will get deeper too? I'm just curious. Anyway, I'm excited about it, but a little nervous. Changes aren't always easy for me, even the good ones. I'm just glad You're not taking away my voice altogether. I use it a lot, You know. Thanks for looking out for me as I go through these changes, Lord. Amen.

The Lord is not slow to fulfill his promise as some count slowness, but is patient toward you, not wishing that any should perish, but that all should reach repentance.
2 PETER 3:9 ESV

SELF-CARE

Lord, sometimes I'm so busy—dealing with school, home-work, sports, family stuff—that I don't really take good care of myself. I eat too much junk food. I don't brush my teeth enough. I don't sleep long enough at night. I have to be reminded to take a bath. It's not that I'm lazy, Lord. I'm just busy! But help me to remember that You care about my health. You want me to grow up strong. That means I have to stop and pay attention to the basics, like eating healthy food and getting a good night's sleep. You loved me enough to create me in Your image, Lord. Now I will do my best to take care of this body You gave me. Amen.

None of us hate our own bodies. We provide for them and take good care of them, just as Christ does for the church.
Ephesians 5:29 CEV

GROWING UP TOO FAST

Lord, sometimes I feel like I'm growing up *way* too fast. I want to be like the older boys, to have the cool clothes and shoes. I want to look and act older than I am. I want to watch the TV shows the big kids watch and play the video games they play, no parents allowed! But You're not in a big hurry for me to grow up. In fact, You have all sorts of things to teach me while I'm still young. So I'll stop trying to rush things. I'll settle in and be a kid for a while. I won't even argue when Dad says, "No, you can't play that video game!" There will be plenty of time to be grown-up later. For now, I'll go on being a kid. Amen.

*Jesus said, "Let the little children come to me,
and do not hinder them, for the kingdom
of heaven belongs to such as these."*
MATTHEW 19:14 NIV

A LIFELONG JOURNEY

Lord I've been thinking about what my life will be like when I'm older. I don't know what company I'll work for or what kind of job I'll do. I don't know who I'll marry or how many kids I'll have, but I do know one thing: I will always be Your son. I'll always walk hand in hand with You. I'll never stop loving You, Lord. That's a promise. I know I can trust You, not just now, but for all of my life. So why would I ever stop hanging out with You? I won't stop! This is going to be an amazing journey, and I plan to walk next to You every step of the way. Thanks for guiding me, Lord! Amen.

Now make me completely happy! Live in harmony by showing love for each other. Be united in what you think, as if you were only one person.
PHILIPPIANS 2:2 CEV

TALL, TALLER, TALLEST!

Wow, Lord. I'm getting tall. It's kind of shocking, really. Seems like every day I'm taller than the day before. I don't mind. I'm just curious how tall I'll be when I'm all grown-up. Taller than my dad, maybe? Taller than my mom? It's crazy to think that my bones are actually growing and my skin and muscles are s-t-r-e-t-c-h-i-n-g. The human body is pretty amazing, if you stop and think about it. I don't have time to stop and think, though. I'm too busy growing. I can't wait to see how I turn out! Amen.

But the LORD said to Samuel, "Do not look on his appearance or on the height of his stature, because I have rejected him. For the LORD sees not as man sees: man looks on the outward appearance, but the LORD looks on the heart."
1 SAMUEL 16:7 ESV

HEALTHY EATING

I'll admit it, Lord—I like junk food. Potato chips. Ice cream. French fries. Snow cones. Brownies with hot fudge sauce on top. . .*yum!* I could eat that stuff all day long. But I won't, because I've learned the hard way that too much of a good thing isn't really good. In fact, too much sugar can make me sick. So next time I'm tempted to drink too much soda or eat too much candy, remind me that there are healthier choices. Give me a love for veggies and fruits, Father, so that I can grow big and strong—healthy from the inside out. Amen.

Apply your heart to discipline and
your ears to words of knowledge.
PROVERBS 23:12 NASB

⫸ GOD'S ARMOR ⫷

It seems like life is one battle after another. You can't let your guard down for a minute! God wants you to be prepared against the schemes (tricks) of the enemy. Satan wants nothing more than to trip you up, but God is on your side, and He has just the right armor to keep you safe.

THE FULL ARMOR

I'm putting on the full armor today, just like a real warrior headed out to battle. You want me to be completely covered so that I stay safe and secure. I don't want to miss one piece of armor: the belt of truth, breastplate of righteousness, shoes of peace, shield of faith, helmet of salvation, and sword of the Spirit. *Whew!* I'm covered on every side as long as I suit up each morning. Above all, I commit myself to You in prayer every day, Lord. I know that life is a battle, but it's one I plan to win with You by my side. Here's to an amazing victory. . .together! Amen.

Finally, be strong in the Lord and
in the strength of his might.
Ephesians 6:10 esv

SCHEMES

I know what it's like to "scheme," Lord. Sometimes my friends and I come up with schemes to trick the girls or to annoy or tease people. We make elaborate plans, intending to catch them off-guard, but it's all in fun. The devil isn't so funny. It can be scary to know he's coming up with schemes—bad ideas or tricks—to trip me up. He wants me to fail. But I'm strong in You as long as I'm suited up in my spiritual armor. Nothing the devil has planned will take me down as long as I'm covered by You. So today I choose to believe the enemy is defeated. I'm a victor, in Jesus' name! I'm mighty as long as I'm wearing Your armor, Lord. Amen.

*Put on the whole armor of God, that you may
be able to stand against the schemes of the devil.*
EPHESIANS 6:11 ESV

BELT OF TRUTH

Lord, I get it: You're trying to teach me how to tell the truth from a lie. Sometimes the enemy will trick me. He'll send people to tell me lies, and I fall for them. Then I get trapped in their schemes. But not anymore! From now on, I want to strap on my belt of truth so that I can always tell when people are fibbing. I don't want to fall for any tricks! I only want to hear and speak the truth. I'm really going to have to pay attention, Lord, so stick with me all the way. Don't let me stumble and fall. With You I can have a truthful journey all the way. Amen.

"And you will know the truth,
and the truth will set you free."
JOHN 8:32 ESV

BREASTPLATE OF RIGHTEOUSNESS

Lord, when I was a little kid, I thought I had to be perfect. I tried so hard—oh boy, did I try—but every time I would mess up, I'd feel like a big failure. Now I know that righteousness only comes from You. My behavior can never be good enough to win Your favor. You love me because I'm Your kid. And You make me righteous when I accept Jesus as my Savior and ask Him to forgive me of my sins. That doesn't mean I won't try to be good. I'll keep working on my behavior. But I'm so relieved to know that You're the One who makes me righteous, Lord. Thank You that it's not up to me. Amen.

Little children, let no one deceive you. Whoever practices righteousness is righteous, as he is righteous.
1 JOHN 3:7 ESV

SHOES OF PEACE

Lord, I love to go barefoot! The grass feels so good beneath my feet. I could play all day long without shoes. But when it's time to go to battle, to fight the enemy, Satan, and win the war, I need my shoes. I don't want to get tripped up over rocks or bits of broken glass. I don't want to step in a sticker patch. You want me to be completely safe, so as I suit up every day I'll remember my shoes. They keep my heart and mind in perfect peace. I don't have to worry about sloshing in a mud puddle or tromping on a hot sidewalk. Thanks for keeping me safe, Lord. Amen.

And how are they to preach unless they are sent?
As it is written, "How beautiful are the feet
of those who preach the good news!"
ROMANS 10:15 ESV

SHIELD OF FAITH

Lord, what good would it do me if I suited up and forgot to carry my shield of faith? If I covered myself on every side but was terrified of the arrows headed my way, I might get stuck! Faith helps me out: It gives me confidence. It reminds me I'm not alone. Faith—even a little bit—helps me win the battle. So today I pick up my shield of faith. I choose to believe for a miracle. No matter what I'm facing, I will believe for the best. You're an amazing God, and You've given me courage to believe. I can't wait to see what You're going to do, Lord! I'm suited up and ready—let's go! Amen.

*And without faith it is impossible to please him,
for whoever would draw near to God must believe
that he exists and that he rewards those who seek him.*
HEBREWS 11:6 ESV

HELMET OF SALVATION

Sometimes I suit up for battle, Lord, but I forget my helmet. Talk about dangerous! If I don't protect my head—my thoughts, my mind—things could go wrong in a hurry! I might get scared and run in the wrong direction instead of bravely facing my enemy. When I put on that helmet, I remember that Jesus has already won the war. He's my defender, my salvation. He guards my thoughts and reminds me that no weapon formed against me will prosper. I'm strong in Him! The enemy can mess with me all he likes, but he's not a winner. . .God is! I don't have to doubt. I don't have to wonder. I can be sure of the fact that victory is coming. Amen!

*And take the helmet of salvation, and the
sword of the Spirit, which is the word of God.*
EPHESIANS 6:17 ESV

SWORD OF THE SPIRIT

Lord, I proudly take the sword of the Spirit—Your Word, the Holy Bible—and use it as my weapon today! It's loaded with verses to keep me focused on You. Whenever the enemy tells me I'm defeated, I say, "If God is for us, who can be against us?" (Romans 8:31 ESV). When the enemy says, "No one loves you," I'll say, "Nothing. . .will be able to separate [me] from the love of God in Christ Jesus" (Romans 8:39 ESV). Every time Satan swings his invisible sword, I'll block him with the Word of God, and I'll win every time, because "greater is he who is in [me] than he who is in the world" (1 John 4:4 NASB). How I love Your Word, Lord! What an amazing weapon it is. Amen.

For the word of God is living and active, sharper than any two-edged sword, piercing to the division of soul and of spirit, of joints and of marrow, and discerning the thoughts and intentions of the heart.
HEBREWS 4:12 ESV

PRAYER

Prayer is an amazing weapon, Lord! Whenever I feel like I'm losing the battle, I just have to talk to You about it. You'll give me plans—strategies—to take down my opponent. I won't ever have to worry. All I need to do is have a meeting with You and You'll give me the best advice. It's amazing to think that the same God who created the universe would take the time to chat with me. Crazy cool! So I'm coming to You today, Lord, not just because I need advice, but because I'm Your kid and I want to spend time with You. Thanks for taking the time to guide me, Lord. Amen.

"But when you pray, go into your room and shut the door and pray to your Father who is in secret. And your Father who sees in secret will reward you."
MATTHEW 6:6 ESV

STAY ALERT!

Sometimes I feel like a security guard up on a wall, Lord. My eyes are wide open! I'm peering through binoculars, making sure the enemy isn't trying to sneak up on me. Sometimes, truth be told, I get a little sleepy. My eyes grow heavy. I forget this is a battle we're in. My defenses are down. I forget to put on my armor. Then I wonder why the enemy sneaks in. I need to stay alert, to keep wide awake. I can do this by suiting up in my armor daily and praying for Your protection—over my life, my family, my friends, and my home. What a great security guard I'll be, Lord, as long as I stay alert! Amen.

"Watch and pray that you may not enter into temptation. The spirit indeed is willing, but the flesh is weak."
MATTHEW 26:41 ESV

⁑ WISE GUYS ⁑

You spend so many years studying, studying, studying. . .all to get smarter, smarter, smarter. But what good would it do you to become brilliant if you weren't also wise? Some of the smartest people in the world aren't very wise, after all. And some of the wisest aren't terribly smart. Is there a difference between "smart" and "wise"? Yes, and God wants you to understand so that you can be both!

THE WISE GUY

I know there's a difference between being smart and being wise, Lord. I can get smarter and smarter by studying, but wisdom (real wisdom) comes from spending time with You. It comes from reading Your Word and praying, praying, praying. If I want to learn how to make good decisions, how to treat others kindly, or how to live a godly life, then I need to hang out with You. You'll give me wisdom to know right from wrong, to make excellent choices, and to be the best me I can be. So make me a wise guy, I pray. Amen.

⁂ ⁑ ⁑ ⁂

How much better to get wisdom than gold! To get understanding is to be chosen rather than silver.
PROVERBS 16:16 ESV

ASKING FOR MORE

The Bible says I can ask for more wisdom, Lord, so I'm asking. I'm not talking about book smarts; I'm talking about the kind of wisdom that comes from You. I want to be wise so that I can follow after You all the days of my life. Give me more wisdom, I pray. Wisdom to make good choices. Wisdom to follow the right leaders. Wisdom to lead others, when the time comes. I need wisdom for school and my classes, wisdom for decisions, and wisdom to know which friends I should be hanging out with. So give me more, I pray, and I'll use it wisely! Amen.

If any of you lacks wisdom, let him ask God, who gives generously to all without reproach, and it will be given him.
JAMES 1:5 ESV

A WISE MAN TAKES ADVICE

I usually feel like I'm right, Lord, and others are wrong. I think I'm the wise one. I don't take the time to really figure out who's right. I just assume I am. But Your Word says that a wise man—or kid—takes advice. He doesn't just assume he's always right. I'll admit, it's not easy to humble myself and say, "Hey, I might not be right this time." Maybe it's time for me to learn to do that. And while I'm at it, I'll also admit that sometimes I need advice—from parents, grandparents, teachers, friends, and so on. I don't have all the answers, Lord, but You do. Help me to listen carefully to Your voice too.

The way of a fool is right in his own eyes,
but a wise man listens to advice.
PROVERBS 12:15 ESV

A WISE WALK

Every day I can be wiser than the day before. That's so cool to think about. Every step I take can be a wiser step than the one I took before it. I'm always learning and growing. So I won't hang on to the mistakes of the past. I've made lots of them. I'll forgive myself for the times I got it wrong, and I'll move forward from here, ready to learn and grow. I'll take to heart what I'm learning and be ready to share it with others so they can learn and grow too. Thanks for teaching me how to walk wisely, Lord. Every step brings me one step closer to wisdom. Amen.

Look carefully then how you walk, not as unwise but as wise, making the best use of the time, because the days are evil. Therefore do not be foolish, but understand what the will of the Lord is.
EPHESIANS 5:15–17 ESV

AN ACTIVE BRAIN

My brain is always on the go, Lord! I feel like my thoughts are going a hundred miles an hour sometimes. And I don't slow down long enough to really think things through. Sometimes I make decisions without giving much thought to them. Then I wonder why things don't work out. Today You're saying, "Slow down, kid." You're asking me to quiet my thoughts so that I can hear Your still, small voice. It's not going to be easy to slow down this brain of mine, but I'll give it my best shot. I want to grow wise, and that means I need to focus, focus, focus on You. Thanks for helping me do that, Lord. Amen.

The fear of the LORD is the beginning of wisdom,
and the knowledge of the Holy One is insight.
PROVERBS 9:10 ESV

WISDOM WITH WHITE HAIR

Wow, Lord! Some of the senior citizens I know are so smart. Seriously! They tell me stuff that blows me away! They seem to have an answer for every problem I face. Maybe that's because they've lived so long. The more time they spend on planet Earth, the smarter they become. This is exciting because it means I'll get wiser as I age too. Maybe by the time my hair is white, I'll be a lot wiser than I am now—it could happen! Until then, keep on teaching and training me, Lord. I want to be a good student from now until I'm old. Amen.

Wisdom is with the aged, and understanding in length of days. "With God are wisdom and might; he has counsel and understanding."
JOB 12:12–13 ESV

WISDOM IN AN UPSIDE-DOWN WORLD

Things are a little crazy out there, Lord. People are doing and saying things that are the opposite of what the Bible says. They're living upside-down lives! It's confusing because people are telling me that bad stuff is good and good stuff is bad. Why are they trying to get me so mixed up? I know what Your Word says—we're supposed to live holy lives. I need wisdom to live right-side up in an upside-down world, but it's not always easy or popular. Will You help me, Lord? Help me to be a right-side-up kid no matter what my friends are doing. Thanks in advance. I'm definitely going to need Your help with this one, Lord! Amen.

Do all things without grumbling or disputing, that you may be blameless and innocent, children of God without blemish in the midst of a crooked and twisted generation, among whom you shine as lights in the world.
PHILIPPIANS 2:14–15 ESV

WISDOM TO OBEY

Lord, I don't know why everyone acts like *obey* is some sort of bad word. It's not! It's actually one of the best words ever! When you're truly wise, you obey because you know that everything will work out better in the end. When I disobey, I always end up regretting it. I feel sick inside, because I know I've done something wrong, even if others don't know yet. I don't like that feeling, Jesus. I'd rather do the right thing and feel good about it than to have those icky feelings that go along with disobedience. From now on, when I'm tempted to do the wrong thing, or when I'm feeling stubborn, remind me that I will feel better in the end if I just obey. My parents are happy when they don't have to keep reminding me to do the right thing. And You're happy when I live an obedient life. Now that's a wise way to live! Amen.

If you will obey me and keep my covenant, you will be my own special treasure from among all the peoples on earth.
EXODUS 19:5 NLT

SILENCE!

Sometimes it's wiser to say nothing at all, isn't it, Lord? Oh, I know. . .I usually think I can fix things by explaining. But I'm learning that keeping my lips zipped often has a better outcome. If I say too much or say the wrong thing, people will think I'm foolish. If I keep my thoughts to myself, they will think I'm wise. So next time I feel led to yack-yack-yack and explain-explain-explain, remind me that silence really is golden. It can change the way people think about me, and that's a very good thing! Thanks for the reminder. Amen.

Whoever restrains his words has knowledge, and he who has a cool spirit is a man of understanding. Even a fool who keeps silent is considered wise; when he closes his lips, he is deemed intelligent.
PROVERBS 17:27–28 ESV

EARS WIDE OPEN

If I want to be wise, Lord, I need to listen to Your still, small voice guiding my path. The only way I will ever hear is if I step away from the noise of life and listen. Most of the time I have the TV blasting or video games playing on-screen. I have brothers and sisters bickering or my favorite music blaring. My surroundings are rarely quiet. But I will do my best to listen anyway, because You're speaking words of wisdom just for me. Today, Lord, my ears are wide open. I'm ready to hear what You have to say. Speak, Lord. I'm definitely listening! Amen.

*An intelligent heart acquires knowledge,
and the ear of the wise seeks knowledge.*
PROVERBS 18:15 ESV

⅃⊪ SERVING ⊪⊩

Did you realize that God gave you special gifts so you could help others? It's true! Serving others is part of God's plan for your life. Who is He asking you to serve? Which gifts will you use? Finding out will be an adventure!

MISSIONS

Lord, I know there are people living all over this big world who don't know You. Some of them live in countries far, far away. Others live nearby, in my own neighborhood. It's crazy to think that some of my own neighbors don't know You, Jesus, but it's true. How can I help, Lord? I can't be a missionary right now, not like the ones who come to my church anyway. I can't move away to Africa or Asia. Show me how to share my faith with people I pass by every day—the friend on the school bus, the woman who lives across the street, the boy who says mean things to me in class. I want to be a good witness for You, Jesus, but I'll definitely need Your help. I want to "go into all the world" and share the good news that You love everyone. Amen.

And then [Jesus] told them, "Go into all the world and preach the Good News to everyone."
MARK 16:15 NLT

VOLUNTEERING

I love to volunteer, Lord, to give freely of my time and efforts to help others. Whether I'm setting up chairs at church or volunteering at a local food pantry, I have a blast helping others. Give me creative ideas, Father. Where do You want me to volunteer? At a homeless shelter? At a children's home? At a nursing home, visiting with the elderly? Maybe I could read books to children at a library. I'm excited about the possibilities. I'll go where You ask me to go, Lord—as long as Mom and Dad agree—and I'll share the love of Jesus with people I meet along the way. Thanks for showing me how to volunteer!

"In all things I have shown you that by working hard
in this way we must help the weak and remember
the words of the Lord Jesus, how he himself said,
'It is more blessed to give than to receive.' "
ACTS 20:35 ESV

SACRIFICE

Lord, I have to admit, I don't always like to sacrifice, to give of myself for others. Sometimes I have to sacrifice my time helping Mom clean when I'd rather be playing. Other times I have to sacrifice my clothes or toys, sharing with my brother or a friend in need. There have even been times when I had to sacrifice doing something fun with my family because of bad behavior on my part. If anyone understands sacrifice, it's You, Jesus. You sacrificed Your life on the cross so that I could live for all eternity. Wow! If You could do that for me, then surely I can sacrifice my time and energy for those around me. Help me, I pray. Amen.

If someone does wrong to you, do not pay him back by doing wrong to him. Try to do what everyone thinks is right.
ROMANS 12:17 NCV

PAYING ATTENTION

I'll admit it, Lord—sometimes I'm not paying attention to what others are going through. Maybe a friend is having a bad day or my mom has a headache. And I don't even notice. Or if I do, it doesn't really change my behavior. I want to be more sensitive to others, Lord. I want to be the sort of person who notices when others are hurting. May I be as kind to them as they are to me when I'm going through a hard time. Today, please show me someone I can pray for, someone who's going through a rough time. I want to pay attention to their needs, Lord. Amen.

But a Samaritan, as he traveled, came where the
man was; and when he saw him, he took pity on him.
LUKE 10:33 NIV

FOLLOW THROUGH

Sometimes the best way I can serve others is by simply following through—doing what I said I would do. Sure, there are days when I don't feel like it, but if I said I would make my bed, I should make my bed. If I said I would put the dirty dishes in the sink, I should put them there. This is one way I can serve my mom, by making her life easier. And I can serve my teacher too. If I said I would finish an assignment by Thursday, I should finish it by Thursday. If I promised to write a paper by Tuesday, I should write it by Tuesday. Part of serving others is simply doing what I said I would do. . .so it's time to get busy! Amen.

If we confess our sins, he is faithful and just to forgive us our sins and to cleanse us from all unrighteousness.
1 JOHN 1:9 ESV

RANDOM ACTS OF KINDNESS

I love surprising people, Lord! Sometimes when my mom's really busy, I'll clean the kitchen or vacuum the living room for her. When my dad is working in the yard, I offer to help. I'm pretty good at digging up weeds. When I see a kid at school who's having a hard time, I say something encouraging. I like going out of my way to surprise others with random acts of kindness. Today, give me creative ideas. Show me how I can bless others when they least expect it. I want to surprise people with my kindness, Lord, and I know You can show me how. Amen.

Do not let kindness and truth leave you; bind them around your neck, write them on the tablet of your heart.
PROVERBS 3:3 NASB

THE GOLDEN RULE

My idea of "do unto others" isn't always the same as Yours, Lord! Sometimes I want to get even. I want to embarrass or hurt others because I know they plan to do the same to me. But You want me to live a different sort of life. You want me to treat other people the way I *want* to be treated. That changes everything! I want to be treated as an equal. I want to be treated fairly. I want to be treated with love and grace. I want to be included. That means I have to treat others that way, even if it's hard. Today I'll do my best to show love and grace to people, because that's what I want them to do for me. It might not be easy, but I'll give it my best shot. . .with Your help. Amen.

"Do to others as you would have them do to you."
LUKE 6:31 NIV

GIVING

You're such a generous Father! You give me everything I need—the clothes I'm wearing, food, a home, even friends and family. I want to be generous too! I want to be the kind of person who sees what others need and tries to help. It's not always easy to give, I know. Sometimes I want to hang on to my stuff instead of giving it away. But You can help me with that. Show me who to help and then give me creative ideas. Will I support a missionary in India? Will I support a child overseas? Can I help out with a local ministry or give to a food pantry? The opportunities are endless. Show me Your plan for my giving, Lord, and I'll gladly obey. Amen!

Now you should finish what you started. Let the eagerness you showed in the beginning be matched now by your giving. Give in proportion to what you have.
2 Corinthians 8:11 nlt

LISTENING

I know, I know! I should talk less and listen more. I've been told many times, Lord. I try to hold my tongue, but it's so hard! There's just so much I want to say and I can't wait to get my words out. From now on I'm going to try to be a better listener. That's a terrific way to serve others, by listening when they speak. I know other people want to get their words out too. So I'll zip my lips and open my ears. I'll pay close attention and not interrupt. I just might learn something amazing if I listen instead of talk. Can you help me with this, Lord? It's not going to be easy. Boy, do I ever need Your help with this one! Amen.

Know this, my beloved brothers: let every person
be quick to hear, slow to speak, slow to anger.
JAMES 1:19 ESV

SHARING THE GOSPEL

I know You've asked me to shine my light, Lord, and I'm trying! In my school and my neighborhood, I encounter some people who don't want to know about You. They just want me to act like them, to blend in. But I'm going to stand firm, Lord! I'll keep on trying even when they make it hard, because I know it's important to You and it's part of being a Christian. I want to be an example, not just to people my age, but to the adults in my community too. Give me creative ideas so that I can shine Your light even brighter. I want everything I do to point to You, Lord. Amen.

"In the same way, let your light shine before others, so that they may see your good works and give glory to your Father who is in heaven."
MATTHEW 5:16 ESV

ᚋ BIG STUFF AHEAD! ᚌ

God has big plans for you, kiddo! *Big* plans! And even though you can't see where the road leads, He can! He's going to take you on an amazing journey with Him. Just stick close to Him and pray every step of the way.

GOALS

There are so many things I want to accomplish in my life, Jesus! I have big plans for myself. I can see it all now! I want to be an excellent student. I want to go to college. I want to play sports or compete in marathons. I want to have friends, do cool stuff, and tell other people about Jesus. There are so many amazing things on my to-do list! I don't know where the road will take me or how many of my goals I'm going to achieve, but with Your help I can do a lot more than I could ever do on my own. So today I choose to give my goals to You. Take me where You want me to go, Lord. I can't wait to see what the future holds! Amen.

᚛ ᚌ ᚚ ᚛

So we keep on praying for you, asking our God to enable you to live a life worthy of his call. May he give you the power to accomplish all the good things your faith prompts you to do.
2 Thessalonians 1:11 NLT

GOD'S DREAMS FOR YOU

I've got so many cool ideas about what my life will be like when I'm grown-up—what sort of job I'll do, where I'll travel, even what sort of house I'll have. My dreams are huge! Then I remember that Your dreams and wishes for me are even bigger than my own. You have supernatural ideas! Wowza! I can hardly wait to see all that You have planned. Today I choose to lay down my wants and wishes and say, "Your will be done, Father!" because I know that anything I dream up is nothing in comparison to what You have in mind. Great things are ahead, supernatural things! I can feel it. Amen.

"For I know the plans I have for you," declares the LORD,
*"plans to prosper you and not to harm you,
plans to give you hope and a future."*
JEREMIAH 29:11 NIV

TRUST GOD'S ROAD MAP

Sometimes I feel lost, Lord. I don't know which way to turn. Should I take this class or that class? Should I join this sport or that sport? Should I listen to this friend or that friend? It's all so confusing. Sometimes I wish I had a map to follow. That sure would make things easier. Then I remember that Your Word is a map! It gives me everything I need to guide me to make better decisions. So today I choose to open Your Word and lean on Your understanding, not my own. Be my guide, Lord. I'll gladly follow as long as You take the lead. You're the most trustworthy leader I could ever find, and I'm grateful to be tagging along behind You. Amen.

Trust in the Lord with all your heart and lean not on your own understanding; in all your ways submit to him, and he will make your paths straight.
PROVERBS 3:5–6 NIV

TALENTS, GIFTS, ABILITIES

I'm having fun discovering my talents and abilities, Lord. I'm not always the most talented kid in the group, but I try! I stretch my fingers on the piano, swing a bat at baseball practice, swim laps on the swim team, or run races. I try lots of things and hope to discover what I'm really good at. I know You will help me find just the right talents to develop, Lord. And I know You're the One who gave me those talents in the first place. What will I be when I grow up: A writer? A professional ball player? A missionary? An engineer? I'm not sure yet, but one day it will all be crystal clear. Until then, help me "grow my gifts" as I practice, practice, practice! Thanks for helping me dream, Lord. Amen.

As each has received a gift, use it to serve one another, as good stewards of God's varied grace.
1 PETER 4:10 ESV

BLINDFOLDED

Sometimes I feel like I've been blindfolded, Lord, like I don't know where to go or what to do. I can't see the signs because my eyes are covered. Then I remember that I can put my trust in You. With Your still, small voice You will lead me. You know exactly which way to guide me. I can trust in You even when all else fails. When I'm in school and I'm confused about a test I'm taking, I'll listen to Your voice and trust You. When I'm hanging out with friends and one of them wants me to do something I shouldn't, I'll follow Your lead. I'm never really blind as long as You're with me, Lord. Thank You for being such a trustworthy leader! Amen.

Lead me in your truth and teach me, for you are the God of my salvation; for you I wait all the day long.
PSALM 25:5 ESV

TRAVEL

Sometimes I wonder where I'll travel when I grow up. Will I go to the Amazon rain forest and see the monkeys and iguanas? Will I travel to Africa to see giraffes, elephants, and zebras? Will I go to the South Pole to visit penguins? Will I end up in Australia hanging out with koalas? All over this great big globe, there are places worth visiting. There are mountains and canyons, deserts and rivers, oceans and beaches galore. And I want to see them all. Thanks for creating this big, amazing planet filled with wondrous places to explore, Lord. I can hardly wait to visit them! Amen.

The LORD will keep your going out and your coming in from this time forth and forevermore.
PSALM 121:8 ESV

THE FUTURE

Sometimes I wish I could see into the future, Lord. I'd like to know what my life will be like when I'm grown-up and what I will look like. Will I get married? Have kids? If so, how many? Will they look like me? Will they act like me? What sort of job will I have? Will I still love the same things I love now, or will my tastes change? Who will my friends be? What will my house look like? Only You can see into the future, Lord. You know it all. I trust You to take care of me every step of the way. I won't be anxious about the future; I'll just look forward to it with great excitement. Amen.

However, as it is written: "What no eye has seen, what no ear has heard, and what no human mind has conceived"— the things God has prepared for those who love him— these are the things God has revealed to us by his Spirit.
1 CORINTHIANS 2:9–10 NIV

YOU GO AHEAD OF ME

I have the best guide ever, Lord! You lead the way. I can picture it now: We're walking down a narrow road, and You're always one step ahead of me so I don't lose my way. We come to a fork in the road. For a minute, I'm confused about which way to go. Then You step to the right. . .and I follow behind You! You're a great leader, Lord. Though I can't see You with my eyes, I sense Your presence when I pray, and I'm guided by Your Word. What an amazing Father You are, always taking me in just the right direction. Thank You for keeping me safe. Amen.

*Then the angel of the LORD went ahead and stood
in a narrow place, where there was no way to
turn either to the right or to the left.*
NUMBERS 22:26 ESV

MOVING TO A NEW SCHOOL

Lord, big changes are coming, but I'm nervous. It's hard to be the new kid. I know You've experienced this too. When Jesus came as a baby in a manger, He was the new kid in town. And He wasn't always accepted or appreciated. That's kind of how I feel when I go to a new school or church. No one really knows me. And sometimes it feels like they don't want to take the time to get to know me. They already have their own groups, and I'm not a member of the club. Help me find my perfect fit, Lord! Show me the boys You want me to be friends with. Help me get settled in, no matter how hard it is. I might be a little nervous, but I'm also excited about what the future holds! Amen.

Fear not, for I am with you; be not dismayed, for I am your God; I will strengthen you, I will help you, I will uphold you with my righteous right hand.
ISAIAH 41:10 ESV

DREAMS

Lord, I have so many hopes and dreams. Sometimes I wonder if any of my wishes will come true. I know You're not a genie in a bottle, Lord, but I also know You care a lot about my dreams. Which ones will come to pass? Only You know, Lord, but I know I can trust You. So as I think about things like what I want to be when I grow up or which part I want to get in the school play or which position I want to play on the baseball team, I'll trust that You will bring the right things to pass. And I won't fret when things don't seem to be going my way, because I know You will fulfill all of the dreams that matter most. I trust You, Lord. Amen.

Commit your work to the LORD,
and your plans will be established.
PROVERBS 16:3 ESV

⫸ HEROES ⫷

So, you want to be a superhero, someone others look up to? It's not as hard as you might think. Just focus on Jesus first and others second. Put their needs above your own. Before long people will be saying, "Wow! That guy's a hero in my book!"

A SUPERHERO TO OTHERS

I want to be a superhero, Lord, one other kids can look up to. I know that starts with being an amazing role model. I want to be the kind of person others admire. When they see me, I want them to say, "Wow, he's really different from the others. He doesn't do some of the things other kids do." I know younger kids are watching my actions, and I don't want to lead them down the wrong path. So give me courage, Lord. Help me to stand strong, even if it means I'm different from the other kids I know. Help me to set a good example, I pray, so that I can be a superhero from now on. Amen.

For the Spirit God gave us does not make us timid,
but gives us power, love and self-discipline.
2 TIMOTHY 1:7 NIV

GUARDING YOUR GALAXY

I'm just one person. One boy. Sometimes I wonder if I can make a difference in this world. I overhear my parents talking about bad things happening—stuff they see on the news—and I see how many people get angry and upset. Some of it is really, really bad. But how can I fix things? I'm just one kid in a great big galaxy. I can't go anywhere or do anything. So maybe the only thing I can do is pray, Lord. I know You have the answers. If I stop worrying—worry never helps anyway—then You can be in charge. And help my parents to stop worrying too. They get so worked up when the bad stuff happens. I promise to guard my galaxy in prayer, Lord. Amen.

Never stop praying, especially for others.
Always pray by the power of the Spirit.
Stay alert and keep praying for God's people.
Ephesians 6:18 cev

A FLEXIBLE HERO

One cool thing about superheroes, Lord, is that they are always so flexible! They can leap through the air and land on buildings then twist and turn and leap again. It's almost like they're made out of rubber! I don't want to fly through the air—unless I'm in an airplane or rocket ship—but I do want to be flexible like that. Can you help me be more bendable so others won't think I'm stubborn, Lord? I don't want to be so stuck in my ways that my opinion is the only one that matters. Help me to become more flexible so that You can use me to do superhuman things! Thanks, God. Amen.

Do not be conformed to this world, but be transformed by the renewal of your mind, that by testing you may discern what is the will of God, what is good and acceptable and perfect.
ROMANS 12:2 ESV

A HERO ALWAYS COMES THROUGH

I don't like when people let me down, Lord. They say we're going to do something together then back out at the last minute. Or they pretend to be my friend, only to turn their back on me later on. No matter how trustworthy or untrustworthy my friends are, there's one Friend who will never let me down. . .and that's You, Lord! You're better than any superhero! You always show up right when I need You. You sweep in and save the day. I don't ever have to wonder if You're going to back out on me. Teach me how to be trustworthy like You, Father. I want to be someone who follows through and does what he says so I can be a superhero to others, Lord. Amen.

Moreover, it is required of stewards
that they be found faithful.
1 CORINTHIANS 4:2 ESV

MARVEL!

One cool thing about superheroes is that they make people believe in miracles! But I know Someone who's even more powerful than a superhero, and that's You, Lord. I love the stories in the Bible about real-life miracles You performed. I wish I could have been there to watch a blind man's eyes be opened or a lame man walk again. I wish I could've seen Lazarus be raised to life again or a deaf child hear for the first time. How cool would that be? I've read in Your Word that You still perform miracles today. It would be amazing to see one firsthand. Maybe one day I'll watch You heal someone who's sick—a grandparent, a friend, or a teacher, perhaps. Thank You for still healing people today, Lord. You think of everything! That's how much You care about Your kids. You're the most super of all superheroes! Amen.

"Behold, I will bring to it health and healing, and I will heal them and reveal to them abundance of prosperity and security."
JEREMIAH 33:6 ESV

THE GENTLE HULK

I hear it all the time, Lord: "Be gentle!" It doesn't come easily for me, not just because I'm a kid, but because I have a ton of energy! Sometimes I feel like the Hulk, knocking over everything in my path. I don't mean to, honest! It just happens! Gentleness is something I have to work on. Show me how to be gentler—with my words, my actions, and my attitude. Sometimes my attitude gets a little out of hand. No matter how others are acting, I want to be a calm force. When they get crazy, I'll get calm. When Mom says, "Hey, cool it in there!" I actually will. I won't react with anger or frustration. With the help of Your Holy Spirit, I'll stay calm, cool, and collected. Thanks, Lord! Amen.

Always be humble, gentle, and patient,
accepting each other in love.
EPHESIANS 4:2 NCV

PASSIONATE!

One thing I really love about superheroes, Lord, is their passion. Wow! They fly into action, ready to get the job done. They have tons of energy and excitement. I need that kind of passion in my life, Lord—not to rescue people, but to do ordinary things like finishing my homework, cleaning my room, and helping out with chores around the house. I don't always feel like I have superhuman strength when Mom or Dad asks me to help out, but I want to! So bulk up these muscles, give me energy and stamina, and help me perform amazing feats (like cleaning out the hamster cage). With Your help, I really can be passionate when there's a job to be done, Lord. Amen.

He put on righteousness as a breastplate, and a helmet of salvation on his head; he put on garments of vengeance for clothing, and wrapped himself in zeal as a cloak.
ISAIAH 59:17 ESV

MADE OF IRON

Sometimes I feel like I'm made of iron, Lord, like I'm so tough nothing can touch me. Then, other times, I feel like a big sissy. I'm scared of my own shadow. I'm so glad I don't have to pretend to be strong when I'm not. You give me Your strength, and I can do amazing things! I can speak to mountains and watch them move into the sea! I can pray amazing prayers of faith asking that sick people get well. It's hard to believe, but You really are that powerful, Lord, and You want to give that same power to me. I'll take it then watch as You do great and mighty things.

"But you will receive power when the Holy Spirit has come upon you, and you will be my witnesses in Jerusalem and in all Judea and Samaria, and to the end of the earth."
ACTS 1:8 ESV

A HERO OF GENEROSITY

I love generous people, Lord! They're superheroes to me. These amazing people are always making sure I have what I need. Sometimes they surprise me with their generosity, giving me unexpected gifts or treats. I love when that happens. . .mostly because I love surprises! I want to be generous like that so that I can be a superhero to others. I want to be the kind of person who gives when people least expect it. Show me how to give like You do, Lord, filled with surprises at every turn. I can't wait to see who we're going to surprise first—what fun this is going to be! Amen.

"Give, and it will be given to you. Good measure, pressed down, shaken together, running over, will be put into your lap. For with the measure you use it will be measured back to you."
Luke 6:38 esv

A SECRET IDENTITY

Some of my favorite superheroes have secret identities, Lord. People in their everyday life don't even realize they're really superheroes. I don't want my relationship with You to be like that. I don't want to hide it away. I want everyone to know that You are the most important part of my life. So no hiding! Everything is out in the open, for all to see. Give me the courage to tell others about You and to share the good news that You, the greatest hero who ever lived, came to save all of mankind. Wow, what an amazing story, Lord. . .better than any movie or comic book. You're the real deal, and I'm so excited to tell others all about You.

But he was pierced for our transgressions; he was crushed for our iniquities; upon him was the chastisement that brought us peace, and with his wounds we are healed.
ISAIAH 53:5 ESV

⫸ AUTHORITY ⫷

I know what you're thinking: *You're not the boss of me!* You don't like to be bossed around, do you, kiddo? Truth is, God has put authority figures in your life to protect you. So like it or not, there are some people out there who must be obeyed! Spend a little time asking God to show you who. . .and how. Before long, it will all make sense.

AUTHORITY FIGURES

Sometimes I wish there were no bosses in my world, Lord. People are always telling me what to do—parents, grandparents, teachers, and others. Sometimes it bugs me that others get to do the telling and I have to do the obeying. But I get it. You're trying to protect me. You want me to be safe, and that won't happen if I don't listen to the authorities—the people in charge—in my life. So I'll submit. I'll do what I'm told. I know that one day I'll be the dad or granddad or teacher. My turn's coming! Until then, I'll do as I'm told. Thanks for the reminder that authority figures are good for me, Lord. Amen.

Let every person be subject to the governing authorities. For there is no authority except from God, and those that exist have been instituted by God.
ROMANS 13:1 ESV

PARENTS

They're my parents and I love them, Lord. But sometimes I get a little tired of them correcting me. I know, I know. . .I mess up a lot. And I hear the words, "Clean your room, make your bed, eat your supper, do your homework, don't fight with your sister," a lot. When I don't feel like doing what I'm told, You remind me that You've given me parents for a reason. They are my guardians, my protectors. They give me boundaries to keep me healthy and safe. You want me to submit to their authority in my life, so that's what I choose to do. I will obey them because it's the right thing to do, and because I know I will be blessed if I do. Thanks for the reminder, Lord. Amen.

Children, obey your parents in the Lord, for this is right. "Honor your father and mother" (this is the first commandment with a promise), "that it may go well with you and that you may live long in the land." Fathers, do not provoke your children to anger, but bring them up in the discipline and instruction of the Lord.
EPHESIANS 6:1–4 ESV

RELATIVES

Lord, I have relatives who sometimes act like they're my parents—aunts, uncles, grandparents, and others. They're pretty good at stepping in when Mom and Dad aren't around and correcting me when I misbehave. Do I like when they scold me? No. But I'm glad I have so many people looking out for me. They're part of the family, and I treat them with respect because it's the right thing to do. Mostly, they just want the best for me. That's why they correct me when I'm wrong, so I don't make the same mistakes all over again. They want me to grow into a young man they can be proud of. Thanks for placing these amazing people in my life. Amen.

Grandchildren are the crown of the aged,
and the glory of children is their fathers.
PROVERBS 17:6 ESV

TEACHERS

Some of my teachers have been really great, Lord. My favorites are the ones who know how to correct me when I make mistakes, but still make me feel loved. They don't embarrass me in front of the whole class or rub my nose in my mistakes. They truly care about me and want me to learn. I know it must be hard to be a teacher, so I ask that You take care of the ones who work so hard. They have a tough job! Show me—and all the other students too—how to treat them with the respect they deserve. Thanks, Lord. Amen.

"A disciple is not above his teacher, but everyone when he is fully trained will be like his teacher."
LUKE 6:40 ESV

PASTORS

Our church has a great pastor, Lord. He's funny and kind and preaches great sermons. Most of all, he's good to people, no matter how old or young they are. I really respect my pastor. He's a great leader. He knows how to visit sick people in the hospital, pray for people who are hurting, preach sermons, tell jokes, and still take care of his own family too. *Whew!* He's a busy man! He teaches us some great things from the Bible. He must have done a lot of studying to get so Bible-smart. Maybe one day I'll be like him. For now, I will treat him with respect because he's an amazing man of God. Amen.

"And I will give you shepherds after my own heart,
who will feed you with knowledge and understanding."
JEREMIAH 3:15 ESV

MENTORS

I didn't really understand this word *mentor* until recently, Lord. Now I get it—a mentor is someone who pours into my life and helps me grow. Some of my mentors have been neighbors, coaches, tutors, aunts, uncles, friends of my parents, and Sunday school teachers. They all work together to make me a better person. I guess you could call them substitute parents because they all care about me like a parent would. I respect all of these people, and not just because they're so good to me. You've given them a special place in my life, and I'm honored to know them. Thank You, Lord. Amen.

Do your best to present yourself to God as one approved, a worker who has no need to be ashamed, rightly handling the word of truth.
2 Timothy 2:15 esv

COACHES

Lord, I've had some great coaches. Some have been super-fun. Others have been tough but fair. I've learned so much from them—not just the rules of the game or how to become a better player, but how to live my life so that others are treated fairly. Maybe one day when I grow up, I'll be a coach. Maybe I'll teach kids how to have good sportsmanship and how to become good players. Until then, teach me how to show respect to my coach on and off the field. Amen.

Show yourself in all respects to be a model of good works, and in your teaching show integrity, dignity, and sound speech that cannot be condemned, so that an opponent may be put to shame, having nothing evil to say about us.
TITUS 2:7–8 ESV

POLICE

Lord, I see police officers all over my town. Some are in patrol cars. Others are riding horses. Some are on foot, walking from place to place. These men and women keep us safe. They work hard day and night, risking their own lives so that citizens in my town will be protected. I respect them so much. They care about the people they protect, sometimes even more than they care about themselves. Their job is dangerous, but they don't seem to mind. They make sure laws are enforced—followed—and they do it all to protect me and my family. I will remember to pray for their safety from now on. Thanks for these amazing workers, Lord. Amen.

*"Blessed are the peacemakers,
for they shall be called sons of God."*
MATTHEW 5:9 ESV

POLITICIANS

Lord, thank You for the people who work in politics—the mayor, city council members, senators, governor, state representatives, and so on. These special people give of their time and efforts so that I can have a good life. They work hard to build stronger communities. They make sure the country runs smoothly. I will treat them with respect, no matter which party they represent. They care about me, so I care about them. I'm so glad You gave them the desire to serve people this way, Lord. Thanks so much. Amen.

Be subject for the Lord's sake to every human institution, whether it be to the emperor as supreme, or to governors as sent by him to punish those who do evil and to praise those who do good.
1 PETER 2:13–14 ESV

PRESIDENT

Sometimes I forget to pray for the president of my country, Lord. He's been placed in a position of authority and deserves respect. I don't always agree with who gets elected, but that doesn't mean I shouldn't pray for them. Maybe I need to pray even harder when I disagree with who's in office. But I want to show respect no matter who wins the election. May my words about the president be kind and gracious, and may I always respect his position, for being president is an honor and privilege as well as a great responsibility. Thanks for the reminder, Lord. Amen.

"He changes times and seasons; he removes kings and sets up kings; he gives wisdom to the wise and knowledge to those who have understanding."
DANIEL 2:21 ESV

⊪ TOUGH STUFF ⫶

You don't like going through hard times. No one does. But the Bible doesn't promise a carefree life. Bad stuff happens, but God is still in control. He won't leave you or forsake you. Best of all, He cares about the very things you care about. He's got this. Don't panic.

HARD TIMES

So many people are going through hard times, Lord. It breaks my heart. Some of them are struggling to pay the bills. Others are going through a health crisis. Some of my friends have even seen their parents get divorced. It's so sad, all of it. I've gone through hard times too, but I know You're always there for me. Even when I want to cry—when my heart is completely broken—You're there. When I'm confused or upset, You promise never to leave me. Today I ask You to bring comfort to friends and family members who are going through a tough season, Lord. Hold them close, I pray. Amen.

⫶ ⫶ ⫶ ⫶

No temptation has overtaken you that is not common to man. God is faithful, and he will not let you be tempted beyond your ability, but with the temptation he will also provide the way of escape, that you may be able to endure it.
1 CORINTHIANS 10:13 ESV

ABUSE

Sometimes I hear stories about people getting hurt, Lord. Like that time I found out one of my friends was getting beat up by his father or that other time when I found out my brother was being picked on by kids at school. I don't like seeing others getting hurt, but sometimes I don't know what to do. Should I tell someone? Should I let my teacher know that the boy next to me is calling me bad names? Should I tell my mom that the girl who lives down the street is crying because of something bad her grandpa did to her? Give me the courage to speak up, Lord! I don't like to be a tattletale, but letting others know about abuse is always right. Help me, I pray. May I never stay silent when abuse is taking place! Amen.

The LORD tests the righteous, but his soul
hates the wicked and the one who loves violence.
PSALM 11:5 ESV

PREJUDICE

I don't like the word *prejudice*, Lord. It makes me sad when people judge others because of the color of their skin or because they dress or look different. To judge someone on outward appearance is wrong. I know that You love all people, no matter what. I want to be like You. If I'm ever tempted to treat someone differently, please check my heart and show me a better way. Help me to love the way You love and to serve the way You serve. I don't want to judge others, Father. I want to love them as You do, no matter how different from me they might be. Amen.

There is neither Jew nor Gentile, neither slave
nor free, nor is there male and female,
for you are all one in Christ Jesus.
GALATIANS 3:28 NIV

WORRY

I'm still very young, Lord, but sometimes I feel like I have worry lines on my forehead. If I'm not careful, I'll be completely wrinkled before long! I worry and fret a lot, especially over things I can't control. I don't know why I struggle with this so much. I know I should trust You in all things. Today, would You please help me lay down my worries? Show me how to let go so that You can take hold of my problems and handle them without me. Nothing is too big for You, Lord. You're an amazing Father who cares about my every need. Amen.

"Can any one of you by worrying add a single hour to your life?"
Matthew 6:27 NIV

SADNESS

Lord, sometimes I go through hard times. I might feel sad, upset, frustrated, even angry. I don't always know what to do with my feelings. I want to jump in bed and pull the covers over my head and hide away from the rest of the world until the pain is over. Father, during those hard times, thank You for wrapping Your arms around me. Thank You for telling me that everything is going to be okay. I don't know what I'd do if You didn't care so much about what I'm going through. Thank You for Your tender loving care, especially when I'm sad. Amen.

"He will wipe away every tear from their eyes, and there will be no more death, sadness, crying, or pain, because all the old ways are gone."
REVELATION 21:4 NCV

THE REPORT CARD

I don't understand, Lord. I worked really hard this semester. Why do my grades keep going up and down? Some days I feel like a good student. Other days, I feel like a loser. It makes no sense at all, but I'll keep doing the best I can. Please help me give it my all. I don't want to get discouraged or give up. If this is a test, I want to pass it! That can only happen if You keep me focused. Maybe one day this will all make sense, but for now I'll just trust You. Amen.

Whatever you do, work heartily, as for the Lord and not for men, knowing that from the Lord you will receive the inheritance as your reward. You are serving the Lord Christ.
COLOSSIANS 3:23–24 ESV

THE BIG BREAKUP

He was my best friend, Lord. My *very* best. We told each other everything—our hopes, dreams, fears, wishes. He knows me better than anyone, and I really thought I could trust him. Then he went behind my back and said something terrible about me. I found out about it by accident, and now I don't know what to do. I feel like punching his lights out, but I know that won't fix anything. Do I act like everything's cool when I know it's not? It's going to take time for me to forgive him. Will You help me through this, Lord? I'm totally confused and don't know what to do without Your help. Thanks, Lord. Amen.

*Give your burdens to the LORD,
and he will take care of you.*
PSALM 55:22 NLT

LONELINESS

I know what it's like to feel lonely, Lord. I've felt that way at times, even when people were with me. Sometimes I feel invisible, like people don't even see me. I try to get their attention, but they don't always notice me. So I stop trying. I give up and stick to myself. Then I get even lonelier. I know the best way to have a friend is to be a friend, so from now on I'm going to try harder to make others feel included. That way neither one of us will be lonely anymore. We'll have each other. Thank You for putting other people in my life, people who can be my friends, my family, my circle.

God sets the lonely in families, he leads out the prisoners with singing; but the rebellious live in a sun-scorched land.
PSALM 68:6 NIV

DEATH

I don't like to think about death, Lord. I know that heaven is a wonderful place, but I still feel sad when I think about people dying. I will miss them so much! Help me not to be afraid of death, Father. Whenever I get sad thinking about it, remind me that one day I will get to see my friends and family members who put their trust in You again in heaven. There, in that wonderful place, there will be no more pain, no more crying, nothing but pure bliss! Thank You for creating a place for us to go where nothing bad ever happens. When I'm reminded of what heaven is like, all of my sadness goes away. Thanks for that, Lord. Amen.

For since we believe that Jesus died and rose again, even so, through Jesus, God will bring with him those who have fallen asleep.
1 THESSALONIANS 4:14 ESV

THE BIG MOVE

This can't be happening, Lord. I thought we would live in this house. . .forever. My friends are here. My school is here. My life is here. Can it be possible that we have to move away? Will I really have to start over and make new friends in a brand-new part of the country? Mom finally got that new dishwasher she wanted, and my room is arranged just the way I want it. My brother is on a T-ball team and won't know what to do when we move away. Okay, deep breath. I'm going to trust You, Lord, even though none of this makes sense to me. I don't know where we're headed, but if You'll go with me, I know we'll be just fine. I'm holding tight to You, Lord! Amen.

For every house is built by someone,
but the builder of all things is God.
HEBREWS 3:4 ESV

ⓘ⯈ EXPLORER ⯇ⓘ

There are so many exciting discoveries yet to be made in your life. So many explorations to go on. Already you're learning life lessons at every turn. (You're an amazing student, by the way.) Before this journey is over, you'll be a regular whiz kid, filled with knowledge!

IT'S JUST STUFF

I have so much stuff, Lord. It fills my room. Electronics. Toys. Games. Clothes. Sometimes I have so much stuff that it clutters up the house, and I can barely step over it. That's when I know it's time to cut back. Show me which things I can get rid of—give to children in need or toss in the trash—so that I only have what I truly need. I don't want to be a collector of stuff. I want to have room in my life for the things that truly matter. Time to clean things up, Lord! Amen.

"Do not lay up for yourselves treasures on earth, where moth and rust destroy and where thieves break in and steal, but lay up for yourselves treasures in heaven, where neither moth nor rust destroys and where thieves do not break in and steal. For where your treasure is, there your heart will be also."
MATTHEW 6:19–21 ESV

SOCIAL MEDIA

I'll admit it, Lord—I'm hooked on electronics. I love to carry around a phone or tablet because I want to be like the cool kids. It's fun to play games, but it's also fun to stay in touch with others. I talk to my grandparents in another state or visit with people who've moved away. Social media can be a great thing, but it can also be a time-stealer. Help me not to get too attached to apps on my phone so that I have more free time to spend with people face-to-face. Communicating in person is so much more fun than texting or messaging, anyway! Amen.

You used to be like people living in the dark, but now you are people of the light because you belong to the Lord. So act like people of the light and make your light shine. Be good and honest and truthful, as you try to please the Lord.
EPHESIANS 5:8–10 CEV

FITTING IN

Sometimes I feel like a puzzle piece that doesn't fit, Lord. I hang around the boys at school and they all seem to get along so well. They're like peas in a pod. And me? I feel like an outsider. Oh, I try to fit in. I do my best to dress like them, talk like them, and act like they act. But it doesn't always work, and I sometimes feel bad I even tried so hard. I know I don't have to work to fit in with You, God. You love me no matter what. I don't have to pretend to be something (or someone) I'm not. With You, it's completely natural. We get along great! Next time I'm tempted to fit in with those around me, remind me that I shouldn't try so hard. You'll bring just the right people into my life, and I'll trust Your timing. Amen.

Wish good for those who harm you; wish them well and do not curse them. Be happy with those who are happy, and be sad with those who are sad.
ROMANS 12:14–15 NCV

PLEASE GOD, NOT OTHERS

I'll admit it, Lord—sometimes I care *way* too much what other people think, especially the guys in the group I hang out with. I wonder what they'll think about my shoes or my clothes. Sometimes I even change the way I talk so I'll fit in with them. In other words, I care too much about pleasing them. From now on, I don't want to worry about all of that. I only want to please You. I'll talk the way You want me to talk, dress the way You want me to dress, and even hang out with the guys (and girls) You say are okay to hang out with. In the end, when I'm in heaven with You, the only thing that will matter is whether I've pleased You, Lord. So that's what I plan to do! Amen.

*For am I now seeking the approval of man, or of God?
Or am I trying to please man? If I were still trying
to please man, I would not be a servant of Christ.*
GALATIANS 1:10 ESV

MUSTARD SEED

My faith in You doesn't have to be huge, Lord. Your Word says all I need is faith the size of a teensy-tiny mustard seed. Wow! A mustard seed is like a little dot on a piece of paper. So even when I'm not feeling completely confident, all I need is a little bit of faith and You will move on my behalf. You'll move mountains if I speak to them. You'll perform miracles! Today I'm using my mustard seed faith. I'm speaking to the mountains in my life—the problems at school, friendship troubles, struggles with my parents or siblings. . .all of it! I speak life and joy into those problems and can't wait to see You turn them around. Thank You in advance, Lord. Amen!

He replied, "If you have faith as small as a mustard seed, you can say to this mulberry tree, 'Be uprooted and planted in the sea,' and it will obey you."
LUKE 17:6 NIV

CREATIVITY

You're such a creative heavenly Father! You made all things—long-necked giraffes, squishy-faced pug dogs, hysterical hyenas, cute newborn puppies and kittens. I'm in awe of Your creation. I love the beautiful sunsets, the sound of the ocean waves, the mountains covered in snow, the fall leaves turning red and gold. What an imagination You have, Lord! Now I know why I'm so imaginative. I'm created in Your image. I want to create masterpieces too, in my own special way. I have a feeling You're going to show me how to do that as I get older. I can't wait to see how creative I will become. Thanks for making me like You! Amen.

"And he has filled him with the Spirit of God, with skill, with intelligence, with knowledge, and with all craftsmanship, to devise artistic designs, to work in gold and silver and bronze."
EXODUS 35:31–32 ESV

HONESTY

Oh boy, this is a hard one, Lord. I always tell people I'm an honest person, but sometimes I'm tempted to tell little white lies. I think I won't hurt anyone if I bend the truth a little. So I tell the teacher I left my homework at home when really I didn't do it. I tell my mom that my sister is to blame for the broken vase when I'm the one who broke it. I stretch the truth when telling a friend something I overheard. I don't mean to hurt anyone, Lord, but it happens. Please help me to be honest no matter what. I know it won't be easy, but it's a better way to live, for sure! And thanks for always being honest with me. I'm grateful. Amen.

For, "Whoever would love life and see good days must keep their tongue from evil and their lips from deceitful speech."
1 PETER 3:10 NIV

HOPE

Sometimes I get my hopes up, Lord. I get so excited thinking about a gift I hope to receive or a trip I plan to take, it's hard to think about the tasks right in front of me. It's fun to be hopeful, but I need to be careful not to put my trust in the wrong things. Sometimes I have selfish hopes. Give me Your perspective, Lord. I want to hope for the best—for a good life, godly friends, a healthy family, and plenty of people to love. Hoping isn't about me, myself, and I. It's about growing stronger and stronger in You. I love You, Lord! Amen.

May the God of hope fill you with all joy and peace in believing, so that by the power of the Holy Spirit you may abound in hope.
ROMANS 15:13 ESV

PROVISION

Life is so great, Lord! Food seems to magically appear on the table. I have clothes to wear, shoes on my feet, a roof over my head. I know, I know. . .my parents work hard so we can have all this stuff. But I also know that You are our Provider. You made sure my dad got a good job. You guided my parents to buy the perfect-for-us house. You make sure I have the food I need every day and the car that my mom drives. Your Word, the Bible, promises that You will take care of us. If I ever doubt that You will provide, don't let me forget: You will supply every single need. That means I'll never have to worry about anything. I'm so grateful, Lord. Amen.

And my God will supply every need of yours
according to his riches in glory in Christ Jesus.
PHILIPPIANS 4:19 ESV

CONFIDENCE

Lord, You know I'm not always confident. Sometimes I'm scared: when I have to stand up in front of the class and give a presentation, when it's my turn at bat, or when I'm at the dentist's office. It's hard not to be afraid. But Your Word says I can be strong and confident when I place my trust in You and not in myself. I really need that, Lord, because life isn't always easy. I have hard days—at school, at home, and even when I'm hanging out with my friends. Thank You for the reminder that I can be confident as long as I'm trusting You. *Whew!* That's a relief, Father! Amen.

Be on your guard; stand firm in the faith;
be courageous; be strong. Do everything in love.
1 CORINTHIANS 16:13–14 NIV

Scripture Index

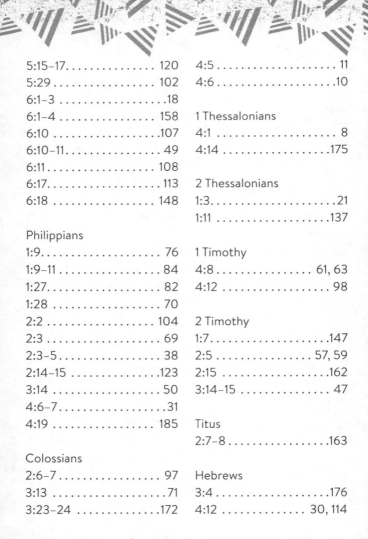

You Might Also Like. . .

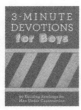

3-Minute Devotions for Boys

Even active boys can make three minutes for God's Word—especially when it's presented in a fun, appealing package like *3-Minute Devotions for Boys*. Created just for guys ages 8 to 12, this book offers 90 readings that speak directly to the interests, needs, and dreams of " young men under construction."
Paperback / 978-1-63058-678-2 / $4.99

365 Encouraging Verses of the Bible for Boys

Every day for an entire year, readers will be encouraged, challenged, and inspired with great passages of scripture—addressing themes of God, Jesus, heaven, love, miracles, wisdom, and much, much more. Each devotional reading will meet boys right where they are—offering words of comfort, peace, and hope for everyday life.
Paperback / 978-1-68322-347-4 / $7.99